As the Saying Goes

A collection of over forty years of wit, wisdom, sayings, signs, poems, short stories, and humor from the notes to numerous published works on the Bible, shedding light on the teachings of God's most holy word, the Bible. There are over 1,100 sayings in this volume.

Ronald A. Brontë

As the Saying Goes

Trilogy Christian Publishers A Wholly Owned Subsidiary of Trinity Broadcasting Network

2442 Michelle Drive Tustin, CA 92780

Copyright © 2022 by Ronald A. Brontë

Unless otherwise indicated, all Scripture quotations are from the King James Version of the Bible. Public domain. All rights reserved. Scripture quotations marked NIV are taken from the Holy Bible, New International Version®, NIV®. Copyright © 1973, 1978, 1984, 2011 by Biblica, Inc.™ Used by permission of Zondervan. All rights reserved worldwide. www.zondervan.com. The "NIV" and "New International Version" are trademarks registered in the United States Patent and Trademark Office by Biblica, Inc.™

No part of this book may be reproduced, stored in a retrieval system, or transmitted by any means without written permission from the author. All rights reserved. Printed in the USA.

Rights Department, 2442 Michelle Drive, Tustin, CA 92780.

Trilogy Christian Publishing/TBN and colophon are trademarks of Trinity Broadcasting Network.

Illustrations by: Nancy Arnold (nancy.pookiebear.arnold1@gmail.com)

For information about special discounts for bulk purchases, please contact Trilogy Christian Publishing.

Trilogy Disclaimer: The views and content expressed in this book are those of the author and may not necessarily reflect the views and doctrine of Trilogy Christian Publishing or the Trinity Broadcasting Network.

Manufactured in the United States of America

10 9 8 7 6 5 4 3 2 1

Library of Congress Cataloging-in-Publication Data is available.

ISBN: 978-1-64773-271-4

E-ISBN: 978-1-64773-272-1

Dedication

To Ms. Lois (as her family called her)

I especially dedicate this book to my mom. People used to say, "Brother Ron, I had a great mother, but your mother was a queen." She was just plain old good. It was often a three-hour visit just because people enjoyed the company so much and could not pull away. She listened, gave good advice, and was just a pleasure to be around. People say I sure was a lucky guy. I agree.

Contents

Preface. 7

Introduction. 9

Chapter One. In the Beginning 13

Chapter Two. The Costs "without" Jesus 19

Chapter Three. Christianity: the Ultimate in Reason . . .25

Chapter Four. God's Will, Yours to Fulfill 31

Chapter Five. Ten Little Churchmen. 37

Chapter Six. Praise the Lord. .43

Pop Quiz 1. Chapters 1–6 49

Chapter Seven. The Real Definition of "Hope" 53

Chapter Eight. Recipe for Truth 59

Chapter Nine. Faith and Doubt. 67

Chapter Ten. Talking and Learning. 75

Chapter Eleven. Avoiding Defeat 81

Chapter Twelve. Emotional Control 87

Pop Quiz 2. Chapters 7–12 93

Chapter Thirteen. How's Your Mood? 97

Chapter Fourteen. How Angry Are You? 103

Chapter Fifteen. Let Us Give Thanksgiving 109

Chapter Sixteen. What Really Matters? 115
Chapter Seventeen. Interactive 121
Chapter Eighteen. The Power of the Spirit 127
Pop Quiz 3. Chapters 13–18 133
Chapter Nineteen. How to Witness to Anyone 137
Chapter Twenty. God's Wrath and His Timing 145
Chapter Twenty-One. How Do You Make the Devil
   Laugh? 151
Chapter Twenty-Two. Are You a Theologian? 159
Chapter Twenty-Three. Give It to God 167
Chapter Twenty-Four. Arguing? 173
Pop Quiz 4. Chapters 19–24 179
Chapter Twenty-Five. Who Was Really Ignorant? 183
Chapter Twenty-Six. Deliverance from Storms 191
Chapter Twenty-Seven. Being Right Is Righ 199
Chapter Twenty-Eight. Our Heavenly Home 203
Chapter Twenty-Nine. Where in the World Are You? . . 209
Chapter Thirty. Why Worry? 215
Pop Quiz 5. Chapters 25–30 225
Bibliography 231

Preface

As the Saying Goes is a collection of over forty years of wit and wisdom from sermons, church signs, friends, original thoughts, teachers, fellow students, pastors, license plates, and wherever the wisdom of the Scriptures is expounded upon. Some are ageless, and some are as original as today as a matter of fact, but all are meant for the glory of God, and it is my prayer that this collection has done so.

This book contains quotes and statements by me, Dr. Ronald A. Brontë. These quotes and statements, as I said, were called from a variety of sources; however, I disclaim that they are all original. Some are 2,000 years old and may contain statements that, in whole or in part, were previously or first stated by others, and in fact, many of the same quotes have been attributed to different individuals, so only our heavenly Father knows who was the first to say them.

Ronald A. Brontë, PhD, 2022

Introduction

Let me begin this introduction with my salvation. From day one, I was reading my Bible, looking through the books at Christian bookstores, finding Christian radio stations, and attending revival meetings. Another thing I began doing was reading the signs in front of so many churches. I'll never forget the first one I noticed. It read, "Become a space traveler, begin here." It was obviously a reference to 1 Thessalonians 4:17, where it says that we will "meet the Lord in the air." I began to copy them down wherever I saw or heard them.

My first pastor, the late Adrian Rogers, was full of quotes, and I wrote about as fast as he could preach. I even listened to him on the radio and took notes. When I moved to another state, I had my parents record his sermons and send them to me. He died in November of 2005, and about ten years later, a book was published with his sayings in them. Most of the ones in there I had already written in my notes.

In addition to that, I record sayings wherever I find a good one: on bumper stickers, T-shirts, in sermons, or signs. Anywhere I hear or see a good one. I hear many on the excellent programs on TBN, which can be used as they are preached. Some I have to reword a little.

Many sayings in this book are original to me. I guess I have the same gift as Will Rogers: the ability to come up with pithy sayings.

I hope you enjoy the following sayings and the humor occasionally interspersed throughout. Most of all, I hope this book draws you closer to Jesus, "the author and finisher of our faith" (Hebrews 12:2).

September 2021

In the begining God created the Heavens and the Earth (Gen 1:1)

Chapter One

In the Beginning

"In the beginning God created the heavens and the earth" (Genesis 1:1, NIV). If you believe this, you shouldn't have any trouble believing anything else.

God's peace is comfortable, but His will is often not.

Wanna know how to miss two Sundays in church in a row? Begin by missing one.

It's only unthinkable if you don't think about it.

The last eight words of a dying church: "We've never done it that way before."

"Sweet bird, that shun'st the noise of folly, most musical, most melancholy" (Bartlett, *Familiar Quotations*).

"Behold the fowls of the air [...] your heavenly Father feedeth them. Are ye not much better than they?" (Matthew 6:26).

Don't just go to church. Be the church.

WHEN GOD IS TELLING YOU, "THOU SHALT NOT," HE IS ACTUALLY TELLING YOU HOW TO HAVE TRUE HAPPINESS.

The longer the wait, the greater the value.

Without tests, there are no testimonies.

Sometimes God will guide you into deep water so He can deepen your trust in Him.

Sin finds you, binds you, and then grinds you.

What if you woke up today with only the things you thanked God for yesterday?

Everything over my head is under God's feet.

The opposite of "truth" is not "error." The opposite of "truth" is "sin."

C h _ _ c h. What's missing? U R.

Everybody Jesus called was busy (take note, couch potatoes).

Death is not the end, just a change of address.

ETERNAL LIFE IS NOT *WHAT* YOU GET. IT IS *WHO* YOU GET.

If it is all of God, we are robots. If it is all of us, we are our own saviors.

Examples of the trinity in nature and the world:
- Space (length, width, height)
- Time (past, present, future)
- Water (solid: ice; liquid: water; vapor: steam)
- Sky (atmosphere, stars, heavens); "the heavens declare the glory of God; and the firmament sheweth his

handywork" (Psalm 19:1).
- Man (body, soul, and spirit)
- Prayer (we pray in the Spirit through the Son to the Father)

Simple question: Why are you going to ask Him to bless you if you are not blessing Him?

One may know Him better, but there's nothing better than knowing Him.

It is better to give people a bit of your heart than a piece of your mind.

Unguarded strength is a double weakness.

Seven days without prayer makes one weak.

Jesus died in our *place* to give us His *peace*.

Sin will keep you from the Bible, and the Bible will keep you from sin.

People do not fail because they

aim too high and miss. They fail because they aim too low and hit.

THERE ARE FIVE GOSPELS THAT PEOPLE READ: MATTHEW, MARK, LUKE, JOHN, AND YOUR LIFE.

We should pray as if it all depends on God and then work as if it all depends on us.

"It is far better to endure patiently a smart which nobody feels but yourself, than to commit a hasty action whose evil consequences will extend to all connected with you" (Charlotte Brontë, *Jane Eyre*, 55).

If it is God's will, it is God's bill.

WE have a KNOW-SO hOpE, NOT a hOpE-SO hOpE.

Evolution is not science; it is science fiction.

The Bible is not a hymn book; it is a Him book.

Synonyms for sin: faults, errors, mistakes, problems, issues, my bad, falsehoods, wrongdoings, shortcomings, white lies, excuses, missteps, misunderstandings—the "excuse" list goes on.

Only one president has used the word "sin" in a public speech: Abraham Lincoln.

The Christian life is like riding a bicycle: either you are moving ahead, or you are falling off.

Don't wait for the hearse to take you to church.

Chapter Two

The Costs "without" Jesus

Without Jesus, hell would be the pay.

Stop telling God how big your storm is, but rather tell the storm how big your God is.

It took God one night to get the Israelites out of Egypt, but it took forty years to get Egypt out of the Israelites (only an eleven-day 240-mile journey).

Fun is like life insurance. The older you are, the more it costs you.

I can prove that there is God. Keep reading, and you will find out how in a later chapter.

Samson was taken down hook, line, and sinker: a he-man with a she-problem.

It's not "Jesus and," nor is it "Jesus or," but it is "Jesus only"!

Sin will take you farther than you want to go, cost you more than you want to pay, and keep you longer than you want to stay.

HAPPINESS IS FROM HAPPENINGS, BUT JOY IS FROM JESUS.

Has your mother ever thought of how difficult it is for you to shut your mouth and eat your food?

The average person makes 3,000 decisions per day, but Jesus is the most important decision you will ever make.

If you put things between you and Jesus, it is idolatry. If you put Jesus between you and things, it is victory.

No God - No peace. Know God - Know peace.

Humility is not thinking less of yourself; it is thinking of yourself less.

Life is short. Death is sure. Sin—the curse. Christ—the cure. Hell is hot; heaven sweet. Sin is black; judgment sure.

Directions for salvation: turn right and go straight with Jesus.

I owed a debt I could not pay. He paid a debt He did not owe.

Until you are ready to die, you are not ready to live.

If your Bible is falling apart, your life probably is not.

ADD A *D* TO "EVIL," AND YOU'VE GOT "DEVIL."

Are you more afraid of sinning this week or of something bad happening?

To err is human and to cover it up is also.

Do you spend more time on Facebook than you do in faith's book?

Y♡u cann♡t always TRACE G♡d, but y♡u can TRUST Him.

"Now, God be praised that to believing souls gives light in darkness, comfort in despair" (Shakespeare, *Henry VI*, 65).

A friend of mine just got back from Louisiana and brought me some alligator meat, but all I have is a crock-pot.

"It is for God to punish wicked people. We should learn to forgive" (Emily Brontë, *Wuthering Heights*, 45).

Dating versus Marriage

Are you just dating the church, or are you married to it?

You have to clothe a lie, but the truth can walk around naked; hence comes the expression "the naked truth."

Five out of every four people have trouble with fractions.

SAMSON HAD THE MOST EXPENSIVE HAIRCUT IN HISTORY.

What's down in the well comes up in the bucket.

Your value is not determined by your valuables.

Concerning evolution: my ancestors did not hang by their tails, but a few of them might have hung by their necks.

Those who follow the crowd usually get lost in it.

You were put on the earth to create an eternal legacy, not an earthly one.

If a church isn't supernatural, it's superficial.

The Trinity: try to figure it out, and you'll lose your mind; deny it, and you'll lose your soul.

You can laugh your way into hell, but not out.

"There is no pit so deep that God cannot get you out"

Chapter Three

Christianity: the Ultimate in Reason

If you think Christianity flies in the face of reason, then cover your face.

Salvation is not the opportunity of a lifetime; it is the opportunity beyond our lifetime.

Every day spent on the earth is time spent away from home (heaven).

The term "one another" is used over fifty times in the New Testament. We are definitely our "brother's keeper" (Genesis 4:9).

Faith sees the invisible, believes the incredible, knows the unknowable, and receives the impossible.

In the Bible, the way to understand what you cannot understand is to obey the parts you do understand.

God doesn't love all of us. He loves each of us.

Suffering is inevitable, but misery is optional.

GROWING OLD IS MANDATORY. GROWING UP IS NOT.

Time may bring wisdom, but it is a lousy beautician.

Nothing is more powerful than a surrendered life in the hands of God.

I am the visible part of the invisible Christ; He is the invisible part of the visible me.

You will see how rich you are when you add up everything of yours that money can't buy and death can't take away.

YOU ARE FREE TO SURRENDER TO WHATEVER YOU LIKE, BUT YOU ARE NOT FREE FROM THE CONSEQUENCES.

If you don't surrender to Christ, you surrender to chaos.

Nothing under His control can ever be out of control.

The problem with a living sacrifice is that it can crawl off the altar.

If you bargain with God, you cheat yourself.

Joseph wailed when he forgave his brothers. Tears are a good sign of true forgiveness.

Don't let your dreams get buried with you.

FIFTY PERCENT OF HIGH SCHOOL GRADUATES WILL NEVER READ ANOTHER BOOK. MAKE SURE *THE BOOK* IS NOT ONE YOU NEGLECT.

When you think about a problem over and over in your mind, that's worry. When you think about God's Word over and over, that's meditation.

While there are illegitimate

parents, there are no illegitimate children.

We are products of our past, but we don't have to be prisoners of it.

What do a tornado and a redneck divorce have in common? No matter which one happens, someone is going to lose a trailer.

Money is both a trust and a test from God.

God is not mad at you; He is mad about you.

Never doubt in the dark what God has shown you in the light.

God is real, no matter how you feel!

Retirement is a short-sighted goal. We have heaven as an eternal goal.

God has power *for* all creatures as opposed to power *over* all creatures.

WHEN YOU PRAY, "THY KINGDOM

COME. THY WILL BE DONE," ARE YOU REALLY READY FOR IT? (MATTHEW 6:10).

Good things become bad things when they keep you from the best things.

This one life will soon be past; only what's done for Christ will last.

People who are prepared get the breaks.

EVOLUTION IN A NUTSHELL: "FROM GOO TO YOU BY WAY OF THE ZOO."

Don't let another birthday get you down: gravity will handle that.

Mercy is God not giving me what I do deserve. Grace is giving me what I do not deserve.

"He is no fool who gives what he cannot keep in order to gain that which he cannot lose" (Jim Elliot).

"What's down in the well, comes up in the pump" – (Matthew 12:34)

Chapter Four

God's Will, Yours to Fulfill

God's will is not something you have to do; it's something you get to do.

SERENITY IS NOT FREEDOM FROM THE STORM BUT PEACE AMID THE STORM.

There are those who make it happen, those who watch it happen, and those who wonder what happened.

Those who say it can't be done should not interrupt those who are doing it.

I am every age I ever was. I'm the four-year-old who remembers feeding our dog, Shep, in the storage room; I'm the five-year-old who threw his teddy bear out of the window on the Interstate and whose mother was dodging the traffic to get it; I'm the ten-year-old who hated wearing false teeth and the sixteen-year-old who didn't want to play football, but mainly, I am the twenty-six-year-old who had gotten tired of the wine, women, and song and gave his heart to Jesus. Hallelujah!

The biggest reason for failures is not mistakes but inaction.

To err is human; to forgive divine.

Jesus was as much man as if He weren't God and as much God as if He weren't man.

"GOD IS NOT WATCHING US FROM A DISTANCE BUT FROM WITHIN AND ALL AROUND" (JIM ROWELL).

Prayer for the worried at night: Lord, I'm going to sleep; You stay up and worry for me.

To forgive is to set a prisoner free, and that prisoner is you.

When you stop learning, you stop growing.

WhEN yOU TEll SOMEONE yOU aRE

pRayiNG f♡R ThEM, aRE y♡U REally d♡iNG s♡?

No "for sale" sign in front of me. I have been purchased and at a significant price.

The same church members who yell like Comanche Indians at the ball games often sit like wooden Indians in church.

Try your best to avoid mistrakes.

The church is not to be a refrigerator for saints but an incubator for newly hatched Christians.

It's better to be a dopeless hope fiend than a hopeless dope fiend.

A guy knows he's in love when he loses interest in his car for a couple of days.

WITH GRACE, THERE IS NOTHING TO EARN BUT MUCH TO LEARN.

Success and prosperity can be the greatest of perils because

they tend to dull our keen sense of dependence on God.

Good prayer: "Lord, make me willing to be willing."

Tombstones: it's not so much the dates that are important as the dash.

JESUS'S SURVIVAL WEAPON of chOICE was SCRIPTURE.

When you take a stand for truth, you're going to have a head-on collision with error.

Watch your words. Make them warm and sweet because you may have to eat them.

The first time I went up north, I was filling my car with gas, and the gas-station attendant walked out and said, "How's your oil?" I replied, "We all's just fine; how's you all?"

Anytime you see the word "therefore" in the Bible, *stop* and ask what it's there for.

If you keep doing what you have been doing, you'll keep getting what you're getting.

A meaningful misquote by a little girl in a preschool class, "For God so loved the world that He gave His only *forgotten* son" (John 3:16, hereinafter, emphasis added).

HERE'S ANOTHER: "COME UNTO ME, ALL YE THAT LABOR AND ARE HEAVY LADEN, *AND I'LL DO THE REST*" (MATTHEW 11:28).

Only one more misquote, I promise. The Sunday school teacher said, "Lot's wife looked back, and she turned into a pillar of salt," and the little boy said, "That's nothing. My mom looked back and turned into a telephone pole" (in reference to Genesis 19:26).

Rivers and men both become crooked by following the path of least resistance.

Give God what's *right*, not what's left.

It's harder to hold your tongue than it is to speak your word.

Focusing on feelings leads to a faltering faith.

Chapter Five

Ten Little Churchmen

Ten little churchmen went to church when church was fine. The going got a little rough; then there were nine.

Nine little churchmen stayed up very late. One slept the Sunday morning through; then there were eight.

Eight little churchmen on their way to heaven. One joined the golf club; then, there were seven.

Seven little churchmen, solid as the very bricks. One was asked to be a deacon. Then there were six.

Six little churchmen kept the church alive. One liked to watch football games. Then there were five.

Five little churchmen seemed loyal to the core. The sermon offended one. Then there were four.

Four little churchmen argued heatedly over church policy. One got up and left. Then there were three.

Three little churchmen sang the service through. Got a hymn one didn't like; then there were two.

Two little churchmen disputed who should run the next church dinner, and then there was one.

One little churchman wondering what to do brought a friend to church one day. Then there were two.

Two sincere churchmen each brought in one more; their number doubled, then there were four.

Four sturdy churchmen simply couldn't wait till they found four others. The very next week, there were eight.

Eight eager churchmen, at worship every week, soon encouraged others troubled souls to seek.

The seats in the church were filled with people cramming every pew. May God supply such zeal and love in your church, too (my paraphrase of "Ten Little Churchmen," author unknown, 1956).

By the way, did you hear about the two skunks that went to church? They had a pew all to themselves. As they sat down, one said to the other, "Let us spray."

The Holy Spirit is not for your enjoyment but for your employment.

You will never learn that God is all you need until He is all you have.

People who use tact have less to retract.

Rudeness is a weak man's imitation of strength.

You're never persuasive when you're abrasive.

If there ever was a time when you loved Jesus more and did more for Him than now, you're backslidden.

"TALKERS ARE NO GOOD DOERS" (SHAKESPEARE; SEE PROVERBS 10:19).

Love is skinny when words are many.

Be a friend of faith and a foe of foolishness.

I swallowed a quarter and went to the doctor. He did an X-ray and said, "I haven't seen any change yet."

Study the Bible to know about God. Obey the Bible to know God.

If there is no hell in the pulpits, it will be prevalent in the streets.

You'll never get your point across if you're cross.

Life is not measured by your duration but by your donation.

This is not a proverb, but a guy just left my office, and it feels good not to have to make excuses or hem and haw around about the truth when people falsely accuse you. I think that's what they call "egg on their face."

Some say, "God said it; I believe it, and that settles it," but if God said it, that is all that is needed, whether you believe it or not.

I heard one guy say, "Hey, you got an extra cigarette?" and the other guy cleverly said, "No, man, this is all I've got, and I plan on smoking every one of them. Besides, if I give you one, I will be that much closer to running out, and I don't like doing that. What is an 'extra' cigarette? Is that when the company accidentally puts twenty-one instead of twenty in a pack?"

SMOKING WILL NOT SEND YOU TO HELL, BUT IT WILL MAKE YOU SMELL LIKE YOU'VE BEEN THERE.

Obedience is a duty to be performed, a debt to be paid, a delight to be preferred, and a decision to be practiced.

Whatever we hear from God overrides what we see.

Character is easier to keep than to regain.

Chapter Six

Praise the Lord

Praise the Lord anyway.

Jesus said, "Follow me, and I will make you fishers of men" (Matthew 4:19). If you're not fishing, you're not following.

Sin would be less attractive if you had to pay the wages each day.

If you don't move those feet, nor should you eat.

If you've not gotten over Satan, you're still under him.

If I lead one person to Christ a year and teach him or her to lead someone to Christ and on and on, in thirty years, twenty-five million people will have been led to Christ. Why don't you be that one person?

Whosoever will are the elect. Whosoever won't are the non-elect.

No man can serve two masters, but he must serve one.

CONCEIT IS A DISEASE THAT MAKES EVERYONE SICK EXCEPT THE ONE WHO HAS IT.

People will forget what you say; they will forget what you do, but they will never forget how you make them feel.

Said the Robin to the Sparrow: "I would really like to know why these anxious human beings rush about and hurry so." Said the Sparrow to the Robin, "Friend, I think it must be that they have no heavenly Father like the one caring for you and me."

Demon number one: "Tell them there is no heaven." Demon number two: "Tell them there is no hell." Demon number three: "Tell them there is no hurry."

It's only the life that is lived with the *approval* of Jesus and in the *authority* of Jesus that will bring *acclaim* to Jesus.

Concerning gossip: don't let them use your ears as garbage cans.

"If you can't say something nice about somebody, don't say anything at all" (Grandma).

I asked a preacher friend how many he was running on Sunday, and he said, "Brother Ron, we're running about a thousand, but we're only catching about 500."

Another preacher told me his problem was up-and-down attendance. He said, "They're either up in the mountains or down at the beach."

I had a girlfriend who was a shopper. She liked to go "buy-buy."

Your danger is not in being on the edge of a cliff but in being unwatchful there.

KING GEORGE SAID THAT THE SECRET OF HAPPINESS IS NOT IN DOING WHAT YOU LOVE TO DO BUT IN LOVING WHAT YOU HAVE TO DO.

Wisdom is the gumption to function with unction.

If you please God, it doesn't matter whom you displease. If you displease God, it doesn't matter whom you please.

With sin, you'll get what you want, but you won't want what you get.

MARRIED COUPLES: SOMETIMES, THE MARRIAGE THAT STARTS OUT AS IDEAL BECOMES AN ORDEAL, AND EVENTUALLY, THEY ARE LOOKING FOR A NEW DEAL.

One man wanted to know if when his wife turned forty, he could trade her in for two twenties.

It will do you little good to come to church and act pious around the Lord's table if you've been bickering around the breakfast table.

Quote from John Candy in the movie *Planes, Trains and Automobiles,* "Like your job; love your wife."

Being baptized with the Holy Spirit means He is now resident in your heart. Being filled with the Holy Spirit means He is now the president there.

He who watches the clock will never be the man of the hour.

There are none as blind as those who *will not* see.

WHAT DID DANIEL DO WHEN HE WAS THROWN INTO THE DEN? HE SAT DOWN, OPENED HIS OLD TESTAMENT, AND BEGAN TO READ BETWEEN THE LIONS.

If you don't go to church because of hypocrites, you'll die and spend eternity in hell with every hypocrite ever born.

If you are not saved by the Word, you'll be judged by the Word. If you are not sealed by

the Spirit, you'll be branded by the beast.

You can't give something that He won't give more back.

Sow a thought, reap a deed; sow a deed, reap a habit; sow a habit, reap a lifestyle; sow a lifestyle, reap a destiny.

Sometimes you need "borrowed" faith from a friend when you feel faithless, hopeless, discouraged or are sick, etc.

Joyce Meyer said, "I don't like getting experience, but I love having it."

Pop Quiz 1.
Chapters 1-6

Answers at the Bottom

1. The last seven words of a dying church:
    a. "Go soul-winning and bring them in."
    b. "Make sure the music appeals to all."
    c. "We've never done it that way before."
    d. "Go visit the visitors on Tuesday nights."
2. When God says, "Thou shalt not," He is actually telling you
    a. He is a party pooper
    b. He is concerned about your good
    c. He does not want you to have more fun than Him
    d. Your parents may catch you

3. Examples of the trinity in nature and the world:
    a. Water (solid, liquid, vapor)
    b. The Three Stooges (Curly, Larry, and Moe)
    c. Nagging wives, nagging husbands, and disobedient children
    d. Addictions: drugs, liquor, or porn
4. The only president to use the word "sin" in a speech was:
    a. Bill Clinton
    b. Donald Trump
    c. Millard Fillmore
    d. Abraham Lincoln
5. The Christian life is like riding a bicycle. You are:
    a. Popping wheelies
    b. Either moving ahead or falling off
    c. Airing up the tires
    d. Loaning it out
6. Directions for salvation:
    a. Do the best you can
    b. Give all your money to the poor
    c. Follow the Ten Commandments

    d. Turn right and go straight with Jesus

7. Salvation is not the opportunity of a lifetime. It is:

    a. Fire insurance

    b. Doing good to be seen by men

    c. Going to church on Easter, Thanksgiving, and Christmas

    d. The opportunity beyond a lifetime

8. The term "one another" is used over fifty times in the Bible

    a. When we can be our brother's keeper

    b. When you don't know how to change your flat tire

    c. When you need to borrow some money

    d. When you need somebody to punch you in while you are running late for work

9. God's will is something you:

    a. Get to do

    b. Want to do

    c. Show others how to do

    d. All of the above

10. The way to grow a church when it is dwindling is to:

    a. Offer lottery tickets

    b. Have a smoking section

    c. Invite others

    d. Make the sermons relevant

Answers:
1. c, 2. b, 3. a, 4. d, 5. b, 6. d, 7. d, 8. a, 9. d, 10, c & d

Chapter Seven

The Real Definition of "Hope"

Hope: an expectation that something good is about to happen.

There is no pit so deep that God cannot get you out.

The "never" lie from Satan: "It will *never* happen."

Howard Hendricks said the best way to learn a foreign language is to speak it out loud. Likewise, it is with prayer: the best way to learn to pray is to pray out loud.

Have you ever fallen asleep praying? Don't be so ashamed. What better thing to be doing when you fall asleep?

It doesn't matter what things you are right about if you're not right about Jesus.

The reason that God honors faith is that faith honors God.

We're too blessed to be stressed and too anointed to be disappointed.

DID YOU HEAR ABOUT THE MAN WHO STAYED UP ALL NIGHT, WONDERING WHERE THE SUN WENT, AND THEN SUDDENLY IT DAWNED ON HIM?

There are two messages in the Bible: "come" and "go."

Sunday morning: the same power that raised Jesus from the dead can raise you out of bed.

What lesson did the fish learn from Jonah? You can't keep a good man down.

"ANGER" is ♡NE lETTER away fR♡M "daNGER."

If you don't heal what hurts you, you'll bleed on those who didn't cut you.

Many people give God credit but not their cash.

Many people "sow their wild oats" when they are young, and when they get older, they pray for crop failure.

Invest in heaven. The returns are out of this world.

To understand the Bible, you must ask yourself three questions:

1. *What did it mean then?*
2. *How does it apply now?*
3. *How does it apply to me personally?*

The Lord never said, "I'll show you, then you'll believe." He said, "Believe. Then I'll show you."

THE BIBLE IS GOD'S LOVE LETTER TO HIS CHILDREN. IF YOU CAN'T UNDERSTAND IT, IT MAY BE BECAUSE YOU'RE READING SOMEONE ELSE'S MAIL.

Every now and then, science may seem to disagree with the

Bible, but let's be patient, and maybe the scientists will catch up.

Okay, here it is (cheaters have already found out). Go to the grocery store and buy a gallon of bleach and have them drink it on an empty stomach. Before long, they will know (a tease from Chapter Two).

Four preachers were talking. One said, "I like this translation for these reasons." The second preacher said, "I prefer this other one for these reasons." The third said, "My favorite translation is this one for these reasons." The fourth said, "I like my grandmother's translation." The others were aghast and said, "Your grandmother's translation? What translation is that?" The fourth preacher replied, "She translates it into everyday living."

God's goal for you is holiness, but happiness is a nice byproduct.

True story: last century, a lady was broken down by the side of the road in her Ford Model T. A nice-looking businessman pulled up behind her, got out, and she told him of her dilemma. Within a few minutes, the businessman had her car running like a charm. She thanked him and asked how he knew so much about cars. He said, "My name is Henry Ford, and I invented this car."

Your heavenly Father is your Inventor and Creator, and He knows more about you than anyone else. He created you in your mother's womb (Psalm 139:14–15), and He can fix whatever is wrong with you. No matter the problem, He can fix it. All you, Model Ts, out there, let old Henry Ford take charge of your life, and soon, you'll be running like a charm.

The Holy Spirit leads you, but He never drives you.

Two words that will change your life: "Yes, Lord."

God makes me want to work, and then He does it through me.

If you wanna cheer yourself up, cheer someone else up.

SIGN TO HANG AROUND YOUR NECK AFTER YOU'RE SAVED: "UNDER NEW MANAGEMENT."

You rise higher when you help others rise higher.

Your faith moves the words that move the world.

An ounce of prevention is worth a pound of cure.

DON'T LOWER YOUR ANCHOR UNTIL YOU REACH YOUR DESTINY.

Not to be irreverent, but heaven is a *heavy, happening, hopping holy* place.

Never bring a knife to a gunfight.

Those things sticking out of your back are shoulder blades, not angel's wings.

Chapter Eight

Recipe for Truth

Facts are like a recipe. Truth is like the meal. You don't eat the cookbook: you eat the meal (the truth).

Teach men their rights, and you have a revolution. Teach them their responsibilities, and you have a revival.

God did not call us to sit, soak, and sour but to serve.

"The Book Our Mothers Read"

We search the world for truth; we cull

The good, the true, the beautiful.

From graven state and written scroll

From all old flower fields of the soul.

And weary seekers of the best,

We came back laden from our quest,

To find that all the sages said

Is in the Book our mothers read.

—John Greenleaf Whittier

DEFINITION: COMPROMISE IS WHEN YOU DO JUST A LITTLE LESS THAN YOU KNOW WHAT IS RIGHT.

Acronyms (first letters spell a word):

Basic

Instructions

Before

Leaving

Earth

Pray

Until

Something

Happens

Together
Each
Achieves
More

God's

Riches

At

Christ's

Expense

False

Evidence

Appearing

Real

Christ

Offers

Forgiveness

For

Everyone

Everywhere

When calamities strike, many say, "Why me, Lord?" rather than saying, "How can I grow from this?"

Did it ever occur to you that nothing ever occurs to God?

Let's all make today a "sonny" day.

Stop trying to recycle what God is trying to replace.

When the Holy Spirit saved you, He was on the way to saving someone else.

Idleness is the devil's workshop. Aerosmith sings a song called "Too Much Time on My Hands."

Gossip: "tell" a friend; "tele" phone, "tell the world."

At-one-ment (atonement). At that one moment (atonement), we passed from death to life.

JESUS'S BLOOD IS THE BEST STAIN REMOVER.

Other books were given for information; the Bible was given for transformation.

Still not:

Ye call Me Master and obey Me not.

Ye call Me light and seek Me not.

Ye call Me Way and walk Me not.

Ye call Me life and desire Me not.

Ye call Me wise and follow Me not.

Ye call Me fair and love Me not.

Ye call Me rich and ask Me not.

Ye call Me eternal and seek Me not.

Ye call Me gracious and trust Me not.

Ye call Me noble and serve Me not.

Ye call Me mighty and honor Me not.

Ye call Me just and fear Me not.

If I condemn you, blame Me not.

—Engraved on a slab in the Cathedral of Lübeck, Germany

Wanna have a good laugh? Think of all the things you've worried about in the last twenty-five years.

Don't confuse God's mercy with God's tolerance.

Let God turn your messes into successes.

Edification is not about how much you know but how much you care.

The more you know, the more you realize what you don't know.

The laboratory of faith is our home, but the legacy of faith is our children.

You know you're getting old when you're looking for your phone and you're talking on it (I've done that).

Fear doesn't empty tomorrow of its troubles, but it zaps your strength for today.

FEAR DOESN'T PAY, BUT IT DOES COST YOU.

True faith is trusting God not to do whatever you want but to do what is best.

Read the Bible. It will give you a checkup from the neck up, help you avoid stinkin' thinkin', and eliminate hardening of the attitude.

If Jesus is still in that grave, nothing really matters, but if He came out of that grave, nothing but *that* matters.

"All that is not eternal is eternally useless" (C. S. Lewis).

"Millions of faithful people have been martyred, have lost everything, or have come to the end of life with nothing to show for it.

But the end of life is not the end!" (Rick Warren, *The Purpose Driven Life,* 53).

Faith is taking the first step before God takes the second.

Chapter Nine

Faith and Doubt

Faith grows by conflict with doubt.

A little girl sitting in the front row of the church said, "Mommy, why do we have to be quiet in here?" and the mommy said, "Because people are sleeping."

We do not have a "victim" mentality. We have a "victor" mentality.

A positive attitude finds an opportunity in everything.

You don't have to know "why" when you know "who."

On Satan's attempt to bring us harm, God uses the ax that the devil is sharpening.

"Looking back, praise Him. Looking ahead,

trust Him. Looking around: serve Him. Looking up, expect Him" (service at Men's New Life Center).

Christ in the alphabet:

A	Advocate (1 John 2:1)
B	Burden Bearer (Matthew 11:28)
C	Christ of God (Luke 9:20)
D	Deliverer (Romans 11:26)
E	Elect of God (Isaiah 42:1)
F	Friend of All (Matthew 11:19)
G	Gift of God (John 3:16)
H	Heir (Hebrews 1:2)
I	Intercessor (Isaiah 53:12)
J	Judge (John 5:22)
K	King of Kings (Revelation 17:14)
L	Lord of Lords (Revelation 19:16)
M	Miracle Worker (John 11:47)
N	Nazarene (Matthew 2:23)
O	Only Begotten (John 3:16)
P	Prince (Isaiah 9:6)
Q	Quickening Spirit (John 6:63)
R	Redeemer (Job 19:25)
S	Savior (Acts 4:12)
T	Truth (John 1:14)
U	Unchanging Christ (Hebrews 13:8)
V	Victor (John 16:33)
W	Wonderful (Isaiah 9:6)

X	Exalted One (Philippians 2:9)
Y	Yoke Breaker (Jeremiah 2:20)
Z	Zealous for Souls (John 9:4)

Note: this would be a tremendous help for children learning the alphabet!

An aged Christian lying on his deathbed was in such a state of extreme weakness that he was often entirely unconscious of all around him. He was asked the cause of his perfect peace. He replied, "When I am able to think, I think of Jesus. And when I am unable to think of Him, I know He is thinking of me."

My pastor Adrian Rogers was interviewed by the *Commercial Appeal,* a local newspaper in Memphis, shortly before his death from prostate cancer. Believe it or not, the secular newspaper printed his interview. He said, "If I remain, I am not worried, for Jesus said, 'I will never leave thee, nor forsake thee' [Hebrews 3:5], and if I depart, the Scriptures say, 'to be absent from the body [...] [is] to be present with the Lord' [2 Corinthians 5:8]. So I am in a win-win situation. Whether I live or die, He is with me" (hereinafter, text in brackets mine).

How's that for a good deal? You can be in a win-win situation also.

Just out: the latest death rate: "One out of every one."

It is better to keep your mouth shut and have people think you're a fool than to open it and remove all doubt.

Heaven is a place of *grace* at the end of life's pace.

The Lord looks not at how much you give but how much you have left over.

A young seminary student being interviewed for his first pastoral job got nervous and said to the committee, "The goal of my ministry will be to raise the devil, heal

the dead, and cast out the sick."

DO YOU HAVE GPS (GOD'S POSITIONING SYSTEM)?

The devil cripples you and then blames you for your limp.

Your absence from the church is a vote to close its doors.

Jesus became like me so I can become like Him.

Knowledge comes from looking around. Wisdom comes from looking up.

Whoever God is to you is He who is through you.

"Faith does not eliminate questions, but it knows where to take them" (Elizabeth Elliot, A Chance to Die, 39).

You don't interpret the Bible; the Bible interprets you.

Satan can't keep God from answering our prayers, but he can keep us from asking them.

Some people only go to church three times: when they're hatched, when they're matched, and when they're dispatched.

On why I preach the Word of God:

- I'm not smart enough to preach anything else, and

- I'm too smart to preach anything different.

WHY DO SO MANY PEOPLE CALL ME "BROTHER RON" RATHER THAN DR. BRONTË? I HOSTED A RADIO PROGRAM CALLED *THE OLD COUNTRY CHURCH WITH BROTHER RON.* WITH IT, I REACHED THE NATION FOR CHRIST. WITH THIS BOOK, I HOPE TO REACH THE WORLD. PLEASE PRAY FOR ME.

There was a lady who sat in the front row of a church. The preacher said to himself one day, "I've had enough of her." After the service was over one Sunday, he approached her and said, "Listen: you get here late, you leave early, you sleep and

snore in the service; you chew gum, talk out loud, and generally interrupt the service." He continued, "Listen: what you do is rude, inconsiderate, and besides all that, you're my wife."

Too often, our churches are "sacred societies" for the "snubbing of sinners" (Adrian Rogers).

At this point in time, we should be more concerned with the destiny of the species rather than the origin of the species.

When God allows the dark to overtake your life, don't light your own fire.

Glance at your problems but gaze at your Lord.

There are many excuses not to accept Christ but not one good reason.

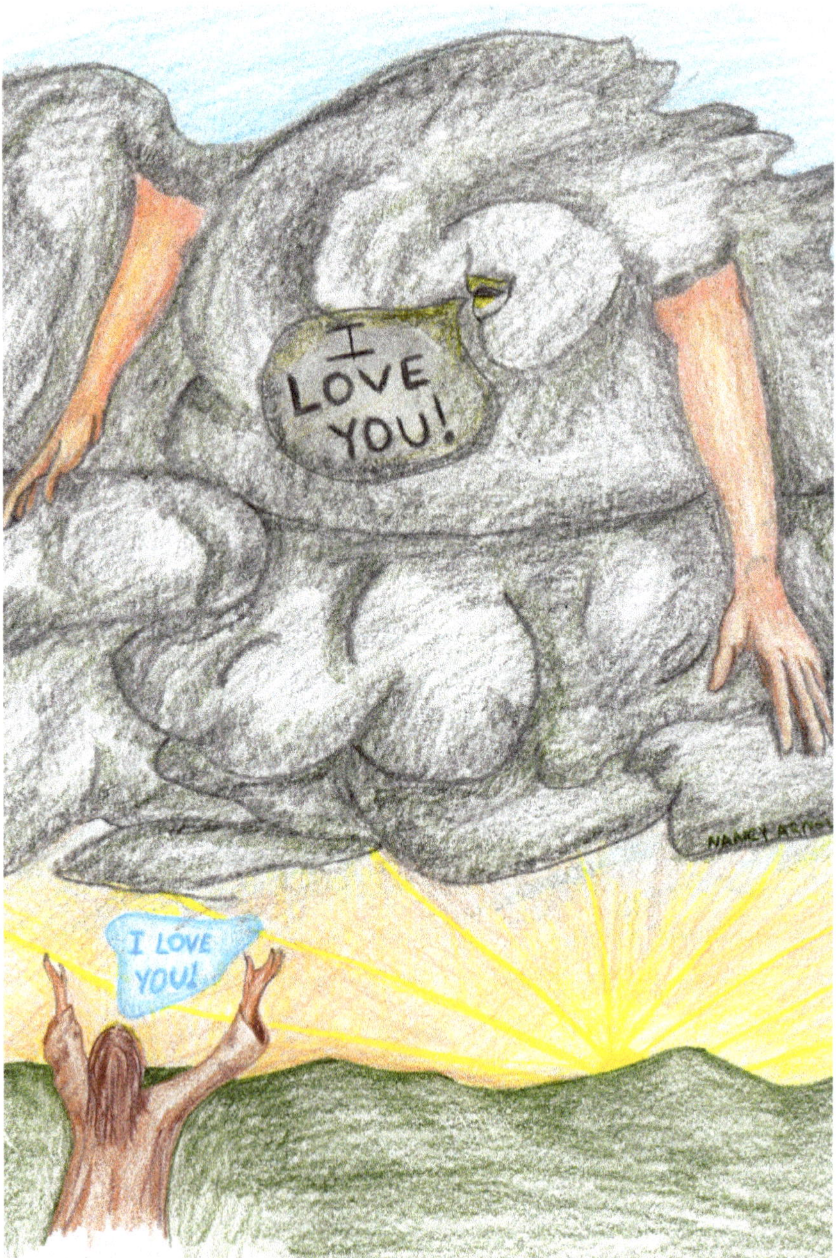
I LOVE YOU!
I LOVE YOU!

Chapter Ten

Talking and Learning

When you are talking, you aren't learning a thing.

YOU ONLY HAVE ONE CHANCE TO MAKE A FIRST IMPRESSION.

Getting old is not for sissies.

If you don't like getting old, there is only one alternative, and it is deadly.

If God closes a door, just keep praising Him while you wait in the hallway.

God does not take all your fears away; He gives you the courage to face the fears.

When life hands you a lemon, make lemonade.

Our greatest witness to the world

is how we handle pain.

THE HARDER I WORK, THE LUCKIER I GET.

The only constant thing is change.

Freedom is not the opportunity to do as you please but the opportunity to do what is right.

There are no coincidences in the life of a Christian.

MaKE This yEaR a REfiNiNG fiRE aNd N♡T a dUMpSTER fiRE.

What we need is not only theology but more kneel-ology.

Engaging in politics is important, but politics never raised anyone from the dead.

Jesus sees through us, and He sees us through.

Prophecy is not necessarily given to tell what the future holds but to tell you who holds the future.

"The Savior Lives"

The Savior lives today! We shall not ask for reasoned arguments—a weary task! When day by day His presence sweetly stills the heart's disquietudes and peace distills in spirits long distraught with sorrow and fear of the unknown tomorrow. Men and angels join to sing Hallelujahs to the King!

—Author unknown

Sympathy: you feel *for* others. Empathy: you feel *with* them.

SUCCESS WITHOUT SUCCESSION IS FAILURE.

It's not how you start the race but how you finish.

"Go ye into all the world and preach the gospel" (Matthew 16:15). Your world begins in *your town*.

Insanity is doing the same thing over and over again and expecting different results.

Winners never quit, and quitters never win.

The master has failed more times than the beginner has tried.

Old proverb: "I once complained that I had no shoes till I met a man who had no feet."

When it seems hardest to pray, pray hardest.

Many people are so earthly-minded that they are no heavenly good.

Your will—your bill. God's will—God's bill.

"These two things hath God joined and man shall not part: dust on the Bible and drought in the heart" (*Sword of the Lord*).

Today is the first day of the rest of your life.

Your insurance agent sells life insurance, but Jesus offers life assurance.

"Nothing sets a Christian so much out of the reach of the devil's reach than humility" (Jonathan Edwards).

Humility is nothing to be proud of.

Humility is an evasive thing: as soon as you realize you've got it, it's gone.

There are over 7,000 promises in God's Word, and He keeps them all.

There are three kinds of people in this world: those who are afraid, those who don't know enough to be afraid, and those who know their Bible.

"If your Bible is falling apart, your life probably is not."

Chapter Eleven

Avoiding Defeat

Defeat is the only prerogative we have when we lose hope.

Christianity is like an oily pole: either you're climbing up, or you're slipping down.

Old Indian proverb: "Don't criticize a man till you've walked in his moccasins."

When you draw the line and then decide to move it a little, there is no end to how far you will go.

Your difficulty didn't come to stay. It came to pass.

The potter doesn't give up on the clay. He just spins it around some more.

Enjoy today. God is on the throne. He will

make all things beautiful (Ecclesiastes 3:11).

God is going to meet our needs, not our greeds. I have needed things that I didn't want. My dad used to say, "You need a spanking."

DON'T GIVE UNTIL IT HURTS. GIVE UNTIL IT FEELS GOOD.

We spend the first half of our lives wasting our health to get wealth, and in the second half of our lives, we spend our wealth to get back our health.

Grace says, "I love you," reaching down. Faith says, "I love you," reaching up.

To *exalt* the Savior, *edify* the saint, and *evangelize* the sinner: that's what we're here for.

The best definition of faith I can think of is this: the opposite of worry. Nobody says, "What is worry?" We all know. Faith is the opposite.

On the way back from a trip, a friend called to say that he saw on TV that some idiot on the Interstate was in the wrong lane, going the wrong way. I said, "One? Man, there are hundreds."

The first time I took a flight from Houston Intercontinental, there was a rare snow, rain, and slush storm. The wings kept freezing, and the ground crew had to thaw them out. Finally, we got off the ground, and a few minutes later, almost instantly, there was the sun. I realized that every day was a sunny day. We just have to get "above the clouds."

Has it ever occurred to you that the sun, "which is light," is pronounced the same as the Son, who is "the light" (John 8:12)?

Can people not hear what you're saying because your actions speak so loudly?

Temper is the one thing you can't get rid of by losing it.

"Evolution"

Once, I was a tadpole swimming in the sea,

Then I was a monkey hanging from a tree.

Boo to religion and hooray for me: Now I teach in college with a PhD.

—Author unknown

EGOTIST: SOMEONE WHO TALKS ABOUT THEMSELVES SO MUCH THAT YOU DON'T GET A CHANCE TO TALK ABOUT YOURSELF.

In all spiritual things, we should be natural. In all natural things, we should be spiritual.

On the things we do: **there are some we need to** *eliminate,* **some we need to** *delegate,* **and the rest we need to** *dedicate.*

The progression of faith:
God accepts me; that's grace.
Then I accept God's acceptance of me; that's faith.
Then I accept myself; that's peace.
Then I can accept you; that's love.
Then you are free to accept me; that's fellowship.

Studies show that women who are a little overweight tend to live longer than the husbands who tell them about it.

Regarding salvation: tomorrow is the only day on the calendar of the fool.

A smile is an act of kindness understood in any language.

Give an act of kindness today. Tomorrow may be too late.

A smile is a frown turned upside down.

It takes twenty-eight muscles to frown and six to smile. Be lazy and smile.

I love rock 'n' roll music: "Rock of Ages, Cleft for Me" and "When the Roll is Called Up Yonder, I'll Be There."

RELY ON HIS INSPIRATION TO CURB YOUR TEMPTATION.

When God answers prayer, it pleases us. When we wait patiently, it pleases Him.

It is your attitude, not your aptitude, that determines your altitude.

If you're looking for a smile today, there's one right under your nose.

Chapter Twelve

Emotional Control

If someone gets control of your emotions, he or she can dictate your actions.

Remain faithful and work hard, and God is liable to keep you around for a while.

Archie Campbell said his wife was on a diet where she lost ten pounds a month. He encouraged her to stay on it. The way he figured, if she stayed on it for thirty-eight months, she would be completely gone.

Where God doesn't rule, He will overrule.

The devil is America's biggest threat, and God is our only hope.

We have "In God We Trust" engraved

on our money, but do we have "In Me I Trust" written on our hearts?

We're not to believe something; we're to receive someone.

What Jesus does with you will depend on what you do with Him.

IN ORDER TO OVERCOME FALSEHOOD WITH TRUTH, YOU HAVE TO KNOW THE TRUTH.

Whenever there is forgiveness, there is suffering on both sides.

Jesus has more fans than followers.

We are not in the land of the living going to the land of the dying; we are in the land of the dying going to the land of the living.

The difference between the Antichrist and Christ is that ♡ne gives me a number and the ♡ther gives me a name. When Jesus c♡mes, will my name be called, ♡r will my number be up?

Growing churches love, and loving churches grow.

The devil would just as well send you to hell from the pew as well as the gutter.

Propitiation: the Greek word that is the equivalent of the Hebrew word for "pitch," which is what Noah used to seal the ark. He sealed it with "pitch" (Genesis 6:14).

It's always too soon to quit but never too late to start.

Crazy thought: "I'm trusting in a God for whom I have no proof to take me to a place I've never seen, but I don't know if He can handle my present situation."

We trust in God for the "hereafter" and the "here and now."

THE PURPOSE OF THE BIBLE IS NOT TO CONCEAL BUT TO REVEAL.

Religion is man's attempt to reach God. Christianity is God's attempt to reach man.

If the odds are against you, remember that God is for you.

The storms don't defeat us; it's how we respond.

Your destiny far outweighs your history.

Do you know where Greece came from? It oozed out of Turkey.

What happens when a pig kills himself? He commits sooey-cide.

We pray without crying, give without sacrificing, and live without fasting. Is it any wonder that we sow without reaping?

One man with God is a majority.

"The ground is all level at the foot of the cross" (author unknown).

The average American between meals is hungry every fifteen minutes. How often are you hungry for the Word? Hint: you can always have it by memory: "Thy word have I hid [memorized] in mine heart that I might not sin against thee" (Psalm 119:11).

IF YOU CAN'T SING, JUST MAKE A JOYFUL NOISE (PSALM 98:4).

If you were arrested for being a Christian, would there be enough evidence to convict you?

While I was in the choir, the music minister asked me to sing solo. I said, "Solo, all by myself?" He said, "No, so low that nobody can hear you."

On the way home, the father complained to his family that the church was too cold, the people were unfriendly, the sermons were too long; he didn't like the song selection, and the choir was too loud. Having seen what he put in the collection plate, his daughter said, "Well, what can you expect for a quarter?"

G♥D SAVES EVERY RACE, EVERY FACE by HIS GRACE (REVELATI♥N 7:9).

Either you will be killing sin, or sin will be killing you.

The less we talk about our troubles, the more it aggravates the devil, and the less it aggravates us.

Pop Quiz 2
Chapters 7-12

Answers at the Bottom

1. What makes sin less attractive?
    a. Knowing that the right type could destroy
    b. Knowing that you would have to pay the wages each day
    c. Knowing that it could destroy your marriage
    d. Knowing that it could destroy your relationship with God
2. What will people never forget?
    a. What you say
    b. What you do
    c. How you made them feel
    d. How many times you went to church since

you were fourteen

3. If I lead one person to Christ and teach them to lead someone to Christ, and on and on, how many more people will be saved in thirty years?

    a. 10,000

    b. 20,000

    c. 150,000

    d. 25,000,000

4. The less we talk about our troubles—

    a. The more it aggravates the devil

    b. The worse they get

    c. The more it ruins your day

    d. All of the above

5. If you can't say something good about somebody,

    a. Tell them something good about me

    b. Make something up

    c. Don't say anything at all

    d. Take off running

6. Wisdom is:

    a. Making up the best thing you can

    b. The gumption to function with unction

  c. Flattery

  d. Speaking your mind so no one can get in a word edgewise

7. When calamities strike, we should:

  a. Sing "Poor, Poor, Pitiful Me" by Linda Ronstadt

  b. Throw in the towel

  c. Cry until there are no more tears

  d. Say, "How can I grow from this?"

8. In "Christ in the alphabet," V stands for:

  a. "Vagabond"

  b. "Venerable"

  c. "Variations"

  d. "Victor"

9. The Lord looks at:

  a. How much you have left over after you give

  b. How much you could give to max out your credit card

  c. How much change you can round up

  d. How many $1 bills you give out of your wallet

10. The Bible:

    a. gives give-or-take advice

    b. is fit for some but not for all

    c. interprets you

    d. is simply good literature; that's all

Answers:
1. b, 2. c, 3. d, 4. d, 5. c, 6. b, 7. d, 8. d, 9. a, 10.

Chapter Thirteen

How's Your Mood?

You can talk yourself into a bad mood, or you can talk yourself out of a bad mood.

Paul said, "I have learned to be content" (Philippians 4:11, NIV). Being content is something we have to learn how to do.

A college student wrote a letter to his dad that was brief and to the point. He wrote, "No mon, no fun, your son." His dad wrote him back a brief letter. It said, "Too bad, I'm sad, your dad."

When you confess your sin to God, you are not giving Him any new information.

God hates the sin but loves the sinner.

The humble get help.

If you watch the old Andy Griffith Show, you will often see the show's doctor make a house call. Doctors don't do that anymore, but I'm here to tell you that the Great Physician Jesus Christ still makes house calls twenty-four hours a day.

Before God uses a man, He breaks him, but Chuck Swindoll said, "Lord, if you don't mind, could you make an exception with me?"

ONCE I GOT A SPANKING FOR SOMETHING I DIDN'T DO. I WAS FIVE YEARS OLD AND WILL NEVER FORGET IT, AND NEITHER WILL YOU IF IT HAPPENED TO YOU, BUT WE'LL HAVE TO ADMIT THAT THE TIMES WE GOT AWAY WITH IT EVEN THINGS OUT AND THEN SOME.

Sitting in a garage won't make you become a car any more than sitting in a church will make you a Christian.

Prayer: the first wireless network.

Is God your occupation or your spare time?

A rich man was asked how much money was enough. He answered, "Just a little bit more."

He died for me so I can live for Him.

Blessed are the flexible, for they are less likely to get bent out of shape.

Poverty can be a blessing, for it can make you aware that you are more valuable than what you are worth.

One man said that whenever he and his wife have an argument, his wife comes crawling to him on her hands and knees and says, "Get out from under that bed and fight like a man."

Another man said that he and his wife never argue, but they can often be heard three blocks away, politely ironing out their differences.

Where there's a will, there's a way.

A LIE CAN GO AROUND THE WORLD THREE TIMES WHILE THE TRUTH IS STILL LACING ITS SHOES.

You can't be right with God and be wrong with a brother.

God made us different that He might make us one.

Overeaters: we are to grow in grace and mirth, not grease and girth.

JESUS IS A GREAT LIFEGUARD: HE CAN WALK ♡N WATER.

If you fail to plan, you plan to fail.

Death is a once-in-a-lifetime experience.

In life, the only thing to be expected is the unexpected.

The other day a bunch of us were standing around, and one guy hollered out, "Hey, it smells like somebody's deodorant quit working," and I said, "Well, it couldn't be me. I'm not wearing any."

"A proverb is a short sentence based on long experience" (Miguel de Cervantes).

If you deny the past, you'll distort the future.

WITH SIN, YOU WON'T WIN, BUT WITH GRACE, LIFE IS GREAT.

With Christ, heaven will be your fate, but if you wait, it will be too late.

Do what is good: it's what you should, but if you sin, you'll never win.

Don't complain about debt if you're gonna keep spending.

Before the coast guard comes on board to rescue you, they ask, "Permission to come aboard?" Have you given permission to Jesus?

There is no rewind button in life.

"IT'S NOT WHAT I DON'T UNDERSTAND IN THE BIBLE THAT BOTHERS ME. IT'S WHAT I DO." — MARK TWAIN

Chapter Fourteen

How Angry Are You?

We are usually angry at someone else's sin because we are committing the same sin.

I asked a pastor, "How many workers have you got in the church?" He said, "Oh, 100 percent of my congregation are workers: half are for me, and half are against me."

"If you could take it with you, it would melt where some of you are going" (Billy Sunday).

It's my business to do God's business, and it's His business to take care of my business.

To complain means you remain.

If you're good to your kids and they complain, now you know how God feels when you complain.

True story: a governor once issued a pardon to a prisoner, and believe it or not, the prisoner refused it. The officials were in a quandary. It had never happened before. The situation went to court. The judge ruled that a pardon is a piece of paper, the value of which is set by the recipient, whether they accept it or not. What have you done with the pardon extended to you?

If you constantly doubt your salvation, here's a good idea: memorize Romans, chapter eight.

NOBODY STUBS THEIR TOES WHEN THEY'RE STANDING STILL.

Attitude: your mental and spiritual response to the circumstances in your life.

An old man once said, "I've had a lot of trouble in my life, and most of it never happened."

Your life is in the hands of the Uppertaker, not the undertaker.

What does it mean when a preacher gets up to preach, takes off his watch, and sets it on the pulpit? Absolutely nothing.

We can never go where God is not, and where He is, all is well.

When you believe the Bible, it's not a leap in the dark. It's a leap in the light.

"There is therefore *now* [not in the future] no condemnation to them which are in Christ Jesus" (Romans 8:1), but there is lost fellowship.

The cancer of worry does not empty tomorrow of its sorrow, but it empties today of its joy.

Nineteen times, in a Philippian jail, Paul tells us to "be joyful."

All sin ultimately is against God (review the Ten Commandments in Exodus 20).

AN OLD COUPLE, HARD OF HEARING, WAS ROCKING ON THE FRONT PORCH. SHE SAID, "YOU KNOW, I REALLY ADMIRE YOU." HE SAID, "HUH?" LOUDER, SHE REPEATED, "YOU KNOW, I REALLY DO ADMIRE YOU." AGAIN, HE SAID, "HUH?" A THIRD TIME, SHE SAID, AS LOUD AS SHE COULD, "YOU KNOW, I REALLY DO ADMIRE YOU," AND HE REPLIED, "OH YEAH, WELL, I'M GETTING A LITTLE TIRED OF YOU, TOO."

When you go around constantly accusing others, you are doing Satan's job for him (Revelation 12:10).

Self-confidence: good; God-confidence: best.

The central verse of the entire Bible, Psalm 118:5, says, "It is better to trust in the Lord than to put confidence in man."

DO NOT CONFUSE WORSHIP AND ENTERTAINMENT. WE OFFER WORSHIP, AND WE RECEIVE ENTERTAINMENT.

If you are not worshipping, there

is no worship going up from your seat.

The King of kings is not like the king at the local hamburger joint. With the King of kings, you don't always "Have it Your Way."

You should keep the faith, but you should also give it away. If not, perhaps you should give it up.

Preaching is not just filling a bucket; it should be lighting a torch.

A guy got up and started walking out during preaching. The preacher said, "Hey, where ya going?" The guy replied, "I'm going to get a haircut." The preacher said, "Why didn't you get a haircut before you came?" The man answered, "When I came here, I didn't need one."

What you do not freely give, God does not need or want ("God loves a cheerful giver" 2 Corinthians 9:7, NIV).

OBEYING GOD IS THE KEY TO HEAR-
ING GOD.

"Speak, God, your servant listens" is different from "Listen, God, your servant speaks."

Who you are is more important than where you are.

If you don't know where you're going, any road will get you there.

Three-hundred and sixty-five places in the Scriptures, we read, "fear not," or "be not afraid." That's one for every day of the year.

Heaven—are you *trying* to get there or *relying* on getting there?

Stewardship is our time and talents and not just our treasures.

Chapter Fifteen

Let Us Give Thanksgiving

For the things we need, we are to give thanksgiving *as* we ask (Philippians 4:6).

The devil sets you up to be upset.

To follow Jesus was not easy then or is now. The disciples did not have a place to lay their heads.

Don't complain about something you're not gonna do anything about.

When God forgives us of our sins, He forgives us of what we call the *big* ones and the *little* ones.

Sin comes from the Greek word *hamartia*. It is an archery term that means "to miss the mark" (the bullseye). It is the same whether you miss it by an inch or a foot, so in God's eyes, there are no *big* or *small* sins.

Every day of your life was fulfilled in God's book before you even lived it (Psalm 139:16).

Go ahead and have your kicks but realize there are kickbacks.

A GOOD ATTITUDE LEADS TO GOOD GRATITUDE.

The dynamic duo: Batman and Robin. The diabolical duo: the Antichrist and the false prophet.

Our government gives us the right to assemble peacefully but not to form a mob.

Where there is no truth, only power remains.

If we all lived by the Ten Commandments, there would be no need for any more laws.

St. Francis of Assisi: "Preach the Gospel as you live. If necessary, use words."

Let every soul be subject unto the

higher powers" (Romans 13:1). If you disobey the law, you disobey God.

You cannot legislate morality, but you can legislate against immorality.

Immorality destroys your chance for immortality.

Genesis 1 in a nutshell: God blamed Eve, Eve blamed the snake, and the snake didn't have a leg to stand on.

Revival begins not in the statehouse or the White House but in the church house and your house.

I HAVE HEARD THIS ALL MY LIFE. I HAVE NO SCRIPTURE, BUT IF YOUR CHURCH IS DEAD OR ASTRAY, YOU CAN LEAVE OR STAY. IT IS UP TO THE HOLY SPIRIT WHETHER YOU ARE TO STAY AND HELP OR LEAVE AND PRONOUNCE THEM ANATHEMA.

The church is not a museum for saints but a hospital for sinners.

By the way, Paul calls all Christians "saints." I feel unworthy, but I am St. Ron; my friends are St. Rick, St. Mike, St. Amanda, St. Dennis, St. Doug, St. Lewis, St. Franklin, and so on. So, when you see me, you are being biblical when you ask, "How you doin', Saint Ron?"

The wages of sin is death, and the pastor of my former church, R. G. Lee, preached a famous sermon sixty or seventy years ago called "Payday Someday."

The church is the only organization besides the Hells Angels where a person must confess that he's been bad before he can join.

When my sister married, she knew one recipe: rice. The recipe was to "place in water and bring to a boil."

If you want what you've never had, you've got to do what you've never done.

After thirty-nine books and thousands and thousands of words, God finished the Old Testament, and in the last chapter of the last book (Malachi 3), He gave a command to tithe and the statement that He hates divorce. Any idea what is important to Him?

God's work done in God's way will never want for God's provision or God's protection.

It is more important to influence people than to impress them.

Scriptural hope is *not* wishful thinking but rock-solid assurance.

MOST AMERICANS' PROBLEM IS TOO MUCH MONTH AT THE END OF THE MONEY.

Did you hear about the wife who asked her husband, "How can we be out of money? We still have checks!"

If you charge your hamburger to that high-interest credit card and make that minimum payment each month, it will take you sixteen years to pay for that hamburger. Is that good stewardship?

"The Lord is my shepherd; I shall not want" (Psalm 23:1). Is that as long as you have Mastercard or Visa?

The last time I had a new vehicle, people saw me and asked, "Is that yours?" and I truthfully said, "Well, it's mostly the bank's."

American manpower begins with boy power (and girl power). Lead your children to Christ.

Chapter Sixteen

What Really Matters?

If Jesus is in that grave, nothing matters. If He is out of that grave, everything matters.

Middle age is the period in life when a broad mind and a narrow waist exchange places.

If you're fifty years old and people call you middle-aged, don't be so upset. That means you'll live to be hundred years old!

"Lo, children are a heritage from the Lord" (Psalm 127:8, NIV), but we all know that in the winter, we were rug rats, and in the summer, we were yard apes.

We are to love people and use things, not love things and use people.

Patience doesn't grimly wait for the end; it anticipatively waits for the dawn.

Prayer is not getting ready to serve. It is the service.

Point people to Scripture, then get out of the way.

COURAGE: A BRAVE WAY TO BE SCARED.

The words "happiness" and "joy" are found over 2,500 times in Scripture.

God grades on the cross, not the curve.

If you grow in the dark, sooner or later, you'll glow in the dark.

WhEN yOU COME TO ThE plaCE whERE JESUS is all yOU havE, JESUS is all yOU NEEd.

I heard an instrumental version of "My Tribute" by Andre Crouch this morning in church and couldn't help but note the first two lines. For the lyrics, visit my Facebook page or website: www.almighty-communications.com.

It is as unscriptural to work five days and be a couch potato for two as it is to work seven and get no rest: "Six days shalt thou labour and do all thy work, but the seventh day is the Sabbath of the Lord thy God: in it thou shalt do no work" (Exodus 20:9-10).

If you're gonna keep complaining about something, don't bother to pray about it.

If you wanna know what the judge is gonna say before you go to court, read John 12:48: "The word that I have spoken, the same shall judge him in the last day."

I played football in high school, and in the first game, I ran a ninety-eight-yard touchdown. I remember the coach being so mad. He said, "Ron, our end zone is at the other end of the field." After that, there were some adjustments, and if not for me, the team would have never gotten any water.

We can do more than pray after we've prayed, but we can do no more than pray until we have prayed.

BIRTHDAYS ARE GOOD FOR YOU. THE MORE YOU HAVE, THE LONGER YOU LIVE.

Education is good, but you don't come to faith headfirst; you come heart first.

I told my friend that a well-known businessman got bit by a dog downtown. My friend asked me his name, and I said, "I don't know. The paper didn't give the name of the dog."

This weekend I had some spare time, so I put my boat in the water. The doorbell rang, and when I got back to the bathroom, all the water had run out of the tub.

WHEN JESUS ISSUED HIS LAST STATEment on the cross, "It is finished," the Greek word was *tetelestai* (John 19:30). *Tetelestai* is a Greek bookkeeping term meaning "paid in full."

You may give without loving, but you can't love without giving.

The hardening of the heart ages more people than the hardening of the arteries.

After all these years, I have finally figured out who was Cain's wife...Mrs. Cain.

Sin is not harmful because it is forbidden. It is forbidden because it is harmful.

Temper is what gets most of us into trouble. Pride is what keeps us there.

Gossip is like mud thrown against a wall. It may not stick, but it leaves a mark.

"Never forget the people you pass on the way up; you may meet them again on the way down."

Chapter Seventeen

Interactive

In this chapter, I thought I would have a little fun. I have listed sixteen verses that many find hard to comprehend. I invite the readers to contact me with their interpretations, and I will put them on my website for all to read. Visit www.almightycommunications.com to leave a comment with your interpretations.

Possible (but seemingly impossible) verses to live by:

> "Be ye therefore perfect, even as your Father in heaven is perfect" (Matthew 5:48). *Can we really be perfect?*

> "Husbands, love your wives even as Christ loved the church" (Ephesians 5:75). Does that mean you would die for her?

> "Let us esteem others better than

ourselves" (Philippians 2:3, paraphrased). I had a man tell me he couldn't do that. What do you think?

"Train up a child in the way he should go: and when he is old, he shall not depart" (Proverbs 22:6). Why do Christian children go astray?

"But if ye do not forgive, neither will your Father which is in heaven forgive your trespasses" (Mark 11:26). *If you don't forgive others, will you go to hell?*

"[...] and Cain knew his wife" (Genesis 4:17). *Where did she come from? Nothing is mentioned about any other humans on the earth.*

"Faith without works is dead" (James 2:20). Must you combine works and faith?

"By the deeds of the law there shall no flesh be justified" (Romans 3:20). *Are we saved by grace or grace and works?*

"If any man come to me, and hate not his father and mother, and wife and children, and brethren, and sisters, yea, and his own life also, he cannot be my disciple" (Luke 14:26). *Are we to actually hate our families?*

"All things, whatsoever ye shall ask in prayer [in my name] believing, ye shall receive" (Matthew 21:22). *Can we get anything we ask for?*

"Abraham gave him [Melchizedek] a tenth of everything" (Genesis 14:20, NIV). *Is tithing for today?*

"Be baptized every one of you in the name of Jesus Christ, for the remission of sins, and ye shall receive the gift of the Holy Ghost" (Acts 2:38). Here are two questions:

Do you have to be baptized to receive the Holy Ghost?

Does the baptism have to be in the name of Jesus alone and not in the name of the "Father, Son, and the Holy Spirit"?

"Without holiness, no one will see the Lord" (Hebrews 12:14, NIV). If you are not holy (as God is), do you have a chance?

"And it came to pass that the beggar died and was carried by the angels into Abraham's bosom" (Luke 16:22). *Where do we go when we die now?*

"Suffer little children and forbid them not to come unto me, for of such is the kingdom" (Matthew 19:14). *Although Jesus said that none come to the Father except by Him, does this scripture mean children are saved?*

"He that believeth and is baptized shall be saved, but he that believeth not shall be damned" (Mark 16:16). Do you have to be baptized to be saved?

These are questions with no answers. I would like to know what you think about these verses. Pick one out and give me your interpretation, and I will share it on my website. I will only give your initials. I welcome theologians but want to know how good a job I have done expounding these difficult verses…and now, some more sayings in chapter eighteen.

Tell them there is no Heaven!
No... Tell them there is no Hell!
No... Tell them there is no hurry!

Chapter Eighteen

The Power of the Spirit

"But when we are really in that power [Power of the Spirit], we shall find this difference, that whereas before it was hard for us to do the easiest things, now it is easy for us to do the hard things" (A. J. Gordon).

It is related of an atheist who was dying that he appeared very uncomfortable, very unhappy, and frightened. Another atheist said to him, "Don't be afraid. Hold on, man. Hold on to the last." The dying man said, "That is what I want to do, but tell me what to hold on to."

Where my mind is, my feet will follow.

A rich man is poor when he has no treasure in heaven.

There are only two places where there is no hope. One is in hell because there you've lost hope. The other is in heaven because there, you don't need hope.

There are three yous:

1. The you that you know

2. The you that you let everybody else know

3. The you that only God knows

We are in the world but not of the world.

What is popular is not always right; what is right is not always popular.

Stand for nothing, and you'll fall for anything.

Courage is the desire *and ability* to do the will of God.

WORRY IS PULLING TOMORROW'S CLOUDS OVER TODAY'S SUNSHINE.

Do the best you can until you know better. Then when you know better, do better.

The best prayer you can pray is one I've prayed every day: "Lord, may this be a totally Spirit-led day." How can you go wrong with that?

A little faith will get you to God. A great faith will bring heaven to your soul.

Where there is light, there are bugs.

Death is only a comma to a Christian, not a period.

We don't need isolation from evil: we need insulation from it.

If you feel your prayers go no higher than the ceiling, God is under the ceiling also.

What you think and say should be the same as what you do.

One of the most tragic things in life is unan-

swered prayers that went unasked.

Works don't lead us to heaven; they follow us to heaven.

THERE ARE THREE KINDS OF CHURCH MEMBERS: EFFECTIVE, INEFFECTIVE, AND DEFECTIVE.

If the cookie doesn't crumble to suit you, try the bread of life.

Jesus is the bread of life, so don't be loafing around.

Steps of salvation defined by D. C. Moody (as quoted in *Sword Scrapbook*, 213):

Repentance—a change of mind; new mind about God.

Conversion—a change of life; new life from God.

Regeneration—a change of nature; new heart from God.

Adoption—a change of family; a new relationship toward God.

Sanctification—a change of service: separation unto God.

Glorification—a change of place; new condition with God.

We are found to find another. We are told to tell another. We are won to win another. We are saved to save another.

"Lead Me to Some Soul Today"

Lord, lead me to some soul today, oh, teach me, Lord, just what to say. Friends of mine are lost in sin and cannot find their way. Few there are that seem to care, and few there are who pray! Melt my heart and fill my life, give me one soul today. – Will Houghton

The Pharisee thought he was perfect. The prostitute thought she was imperfect. Jesus says we're all the same (Romans 3:23).

It's not what you know; it's who you know.

Five of the greatest words on the earth: "How can I help you?"

Prayer: "The joy You provide is my strength, Dear God. Help me be a messenger to others."

Pop Quiz 3. Chapters 13-18

Answers at the Bottom

1. Paul said,
    a. "I can be content with a lot of money."
    b. "I can be content with a big house."
    c. "I can be content with fame and fortune."
    d. "I can be content with what I have."

2. If you fail to plan:
    a. You plan to fail
    b. You better get lucky
    c. Get someone else to plan for you
    d. You just need to give up

3. When you believe the Bible,
    a. It's an ignorant man's crutch
    b. It's a leap in the light
    c. You need to have your head examined
    d. You apparently flunked out of grade school

4. God loveth a _____ giver.
   a. grudging
   b. sometimes
   c. cheerful
   d. dishonest

5. A good attitude leads to:
   a. Unrealistic expectations
   b. Good gratitude
   c. A lot of moocher friends
   d. An early death

6. The church is not a museum for saints, but
   a. A hospital for sinners
   b. Good business contacts
   c. A place to show off your new hat
   d. A place to get a good Sunday-morning nap

7. Patience anticipatively waits for:
   a. Your death
   b. You being locked up in a nuthouse
   c. The dawn
   d. You to forget about the problem

8. When you come to the place where Jesus is all you have, Jesus is
    a. usually out of town
    b. too busy with his friends
    c. all you need
    d. taking the day off

9. Bible education is good, but you don't come head-first. You come _____ first:
    a. feet
    b. hands
    c. heart
    d. stomach

10. I need other books. The Bible _____:
    a. is too difficult
    b. has too many translations
    c. is not relevant now
    d. reads me

Answers: 1. d, 2. a, 3. b, 4. c, 5. b, 6. a, 7. c, 8. c, 9. c, 10. d

Chapter Nineteen

How to Witness to Anyone

You can witness to anyone. Barbara Walters wrote a book titled *How to Talk with Practically Anybody about Practically Anything*. It would be a good tool for those wanting to be soul winners.

Let your smile be a window of hope, reflecting God's love. One day I rode in an ice-cream truck, and what an uplift at the end of the day to have seen so many smiling faces it was.

A proverb is a saying, specifically instructed and generally followed.

Will Rogers said, "I never met a man I didn't like." There is some good in everyone.

Truth has only to change hands a few times to become fiction.

There's nothing wrong in having nothing to say unless you insist on saying it.

When a little success turns a man's head, it invariably causes pain in the neck to others.

"Cowardice asks, 'Is it safe?' Expediency asks, 'Is it polite?' Vanity asks, 'Is it popular?' But conscience asks, 'Is it right?'" (William Morley Punshon).

A PHILOSOPHER SEES LESS ON HIS TIPTOES THAN A CHRISTIAN ON HIS KNEES!

What was the fruit in the garden of Eden? Figs. "They sewed *fig* leaves together" (Genesis 3:7).

Keep your lamp burning and let God place it where He will.

Sin's smiles are more dangerous than its frowns.

Service is love in overalls.

To touch another heart, you must use your own.

What we give determines our wealth, not what we get.

A church is never a place but always a people, never a fold but always a flock, never a sacred building but always a believing assembly.

"Love is not blind: it sees more, not less. But because it sees more, it is willing to see less" (Rabbi Julius Gordon).

Some churches have a list of don'ts such as alcohol, tobacco, coffee, going to movies, etc., but what about adding to the list arrogance, insensitivity, harshness, indifference, and being critical? Are some sins worse than others?

God casts our sins on as far as the east is from the west. Start traveling east and tell me when you get there.

INTENDING TO BE OBEDIENT IS NOT THE SAME THING AS OBEDIENCE.

Three things God wants to see in you:

    1. Holiness

    2. Humility

    3. Him

A man who did not believe in God did not want his seven-year-old boy to ever know about God. They lived in the woods, but one night, the boy was sitting in the backyard, looking up. The father said, "Son, what are you looking at?" And the little boy replied, "Dad, I think somebody is up there." In Psalm 14:1, we read, "The fool hath said in his heart, There is no God."

The past should be a guidepost, not a hitching post.

FEAR DESTROYS FELLOWSHIP, BUT ASSURANCE ENSURES INTIMACY.

God wants our money because He knows it wants us.

Gossip: Don't repeat it. Delete it.

You can't put your foot in your mouth when it's closed.

Do your givin' while you're livin' so you'll be knowin' where it's goin'.

One farmer's land was so steep that he could look up the chimney to see the cows coming home.

If you have money in your wallet and change in your pocket, you are among the top 89 percent of the wealthiest people in the world.

PRAISE INFUSES THE ENERGY OF GOD AND CONFUSES THE ENEMIES OF GOD.

I heard of a father who was so cheap that he told his son, "Whenever that ice-cream truck is driving around the neighborhood, playing that music, it means they are all out of ice cream."

It's not the length of the prayer but the depth that counts. (Shortest prayer in the Bible is from Matthew 14:30, "Lord, save me.")

Dennis Stoll said, "Alcohol won't change your problems no more than milk or water." Jesus said, "I am the way, the truth, and the life. No man cometh unto the Father but by me" (John 14:6).

Can a fish swallow a man and the man live? In 1926 in England, a man was swallowed by a fish and was spit out after three days. I saw a picture of him. He was green from the digestive fluid and covered with seaweed, but he lived. In the 1960s, there was a periodic TV show called *The Undersea World of Jacques Cousteau*. One of its swimmers was swallowed by a large fish, spit out, and lived. When in doubt, believe God.

A cannibal said to his wife, "I don't like your mother," and she retorted, "Well, then just eat your vegetables."

A cannibal chief was asked, "Chief, just what do you know about Christianity?" and the chief said, "Well, we got a little taste of it when the last missionary came through."

Your prayers to God are answered: "Yes," "No," and "Wait."

Two types of people: (1) Thy will be done; (2) my will be done.

Church: you come here to learn how to act when you're not here.

Thirteen percent of Jesus's teaching was about hell, far more than about heaven.

God does not need your help in judging others.

"When King Nebuchadnezzar threw Daniel in the den, he sat down, opened up his old testament, and began to read between the lions."

Chapter Twenty

God's Wrath and His Timing

God's wrath is not always swift, but it is always certain.

MEEKNESS IS STRENGTH UNDER CONTROL.

When asked about whether telling the devil to leave you alone is not like praying to him: you are not praying to a cat when you say, "Scat!"

There are two classes of people: the saints and the ain'ts.

The mission of the church: make them, mark them, and mature them.

God's plan for your life was conceived in love (Jeremiah 29:11–13).

A boy cleaning the backyard said, "Dad, I've done everything to move this rock, and

I can't move it." The dad replied, *"No, you haven't. You haven't asked me to help."*

We're just nobodies trying to tell everybody about somebody who can save anybody.

IF YOU'RE NOT MOVING FORWARD AS YOU LIVE, YOU'RE MOVING BACKWARD.

Faith is my response to what God has already done.

"Those who don't remember the past are condemned to repeat it" (George Santayana).

God will never love you more than He does right now.

God loves you on your good days and your bad days.

Cheap grace with no repentance is a disgrace.

Behavior modifications will not change you. Jesus will.

When the plain sense makes good sense, seek no other.

Take care of your thoughts when you're alone. Take care of your words when you're with others.

A woman had five sets of twins:

1. *One was a policeman; the other spent most of his time in a police car.*

2. *Of the second set, one was a prison warden; the other spent all his time there also.*

3. *The third was an undercover drug officer; the other spent most of his time in drug neighborhoods, too.*

4. *One was a gun dealer. The other was shooting guns all the time also.*

5. *Of the last two, one was a lawyer. The other spent all his time in court also.*

Which twin are you the most like?

WHEN A CHRISTIAN IS IN THE WRONG PLACE, HIS OR HER RIGHT PLACE

WILL BE EMPTY.

Most people who fly from temptation usually leave a forwarding address.

One cannot successfully walk with the Lord while running with the world.

"The freest man in the world is the man who is a willing servant of Christ. The veriest slave in the world is he who thinks he is his own master, while he is the bond-servant of his own lusts" (Henry Trumbull, *The Life Story of Henry Clay Trumbull*, 462).

In spite of inflation, the wages of sin remain the same.

"Benevolence in this world is not what we take up, but what we give up that makes us rich" (H. W. Becker).

God has two dwellings: one in heaven and the other in a meek and thankful heart.

When a collection was being counted after a missionary's talk, a small piece of paper was found on the plate. It simply read, "Myself." It was given that night by a young man who was committing himself to the mission field (*Sword of the Lord*).

Some have ability without consecration, while others have conservation without ability. Thank God for consecrated ability.

"Jesus never taught men how to make a living. He taught them how to live" (Dr. Bob Jones Sr.).

God's tests are to strengthen our faith. Satan's temptations are to destroy life.

"GO YE INTO ALL THE WORLD AND PREACH THE GOSPEL TO EVERY CREATURE" (MARK 16:15). YOUR WORLD BEGINS IN YOUR TOWN.

A sign I saw hanging over the door as we left the church: "You are now entering the mis-

sion field."

"The greater the knowledge of the enemy, the greater the victory" (General Douglas McArthur).

President Zachary Taylor refused to attend a key cabinet meeting one Sunday morning at ten o'clock. He told his cabinet that he had a much more important meeting with his Father at 10:30 in church.

Chapter Twenty-One

How Do You Make the Devil Laugh?

The devil laughs at our organizations; he mocks our schemes; he ridicules our good intentions, but he fears our prayers.

"The love of wealth makes bitter men; the love of God makes better men" (W. L. Hudson).

Giving until it hurts is not a true measure of charity. Some are more easily hurt than others.

As you have noticed, these sayings and the Scriptures have a lot to say about humility and forgiveness.

Nine characteristics of true humility:

1. Willingness to ask for help

2. Quickness to forgive

3. Quickness to forget

4. Readiness in admitting one's own weakness

5. Always making others feel good

6. Happily serving others

7. Thankfulness

8. A tender conscience and quickness to repent

9. How we treat others

I'm not gonna say I was a rotten kid, but my parents sent me to a summer camp, and when I came back, they moved.

"It's never right to do wrong to get a chance to do right" (Dr. Bob Jones Sr.).

"Be careful little mouths what you say." Many people open their mouths just to exchange "feet."

DO YOU OFTEN PRAY FOR GOD TO DO SOMETHING FOR OTHERS THAT YOU CAN DO?

Jesus is the only person who ever lived who could call Himself humble.

A habit can be broken in thirty days (great movie: *28 Days* with Sandra Bullock).

God did not promise smooth sailing, just a safe landing.

PASTOR (AT THE END OF THE SERMON): "AND NOW, BRETHREN, LET US ALL GIVE IN ACCORDANCE WITH WHAT WE REPORTED ON OUR INCOME TAX."

Two pastors were discussing whether we should tithe on our net or our gross. The first pastor said we should tithe on our net. The second pastor said we should tithe on our gross. "Just how do you figure that?" asked the first pastor. "Because God gets more that way."

The groans we endure are temporary. The glory we expect is eternal.

I'll never forget being six years old and, on Christmas, my dad teaching me to ride my first bicycle. He held the bike a few times, but finally, he let me go solo, pretty sure that I would fall. He was not being mean or cruel. Neither is God when He lets things like that happen to you. "It is good for me that I have been afflicted, that I might learn thy statutes" (Psalm 119:71).

You will never take responsibility for your past till you realize that God takes responsibility for it all.

I mentioned earlier that I played football. I also played baseball. I started the season at right field and ended the season on the left bench.

Everything in your life, to take from the title of the Clint Eastwood movie *The Good, the Bad, and the Ugly*, is allowed to conform us to the image of God's Son.

GOD DOESN'T REVEAL HIS GRAND DESIGN. HE REVEALS HIMSELF.

When you feel fear, confront it. Don't run. It's just like falling off a horse. You get right back on.

God is not for you because you are good. It is because He is good.

Bloom where you planted.

If you take care of little problems, then you won't have big problems.

One time I preached, and a fellow came up and shared, "Brother Ron, your preaching was really anointing," and I said, "Well, thank you," and he said, "No, I said it was *annoying*."

Another time I preached, and later, a lady came up and said, "Brother Ron, how do you know you were called to preach?" And I said, "Ma'am, one day I looked up, and there were two clouds. One formed the letter P, and the other formed the letter C, and that told me that God was calling me to preach Christ. I heard her whisper to the lady next to her, "I think it meant 'plow corn.'"

The only way to not be regretful about tomorrow is to do it right today.

You're always spending time, energy, and money. Spend right.

Once saved, you go to the same as the second coming: in a moment, in the twinkling of an eye, from zero to hero.

Do you have three parents? A mother, a father, and a heavenly Father?

"THERE IS NONE THAT DOETH GOOD, NO, NOT ONE" (ROMANS 3:12). HAVE YOU NOTICED THAT THE OLD GOSPEL SONG (BY GEORGE HUGG AND JOHNSON OATMAN JR.) CONTAINS THE SAME WORDS, "I HAVE NOT A FRIEND LIKE THE LOWLY JESUS, NO, NOT ONE, NO, NOT ONE"?

One word you will never see in the Bible: "lucky."

The problem about living in the past or future: you will miss the present.

Remember that in marriage, the two of you shall become one, but it takes a lifetime.

"Every day of your life was fulfilled in God's book before you even lived it"
— (Psalm 139:16)

Chapter Twenty-Two

Are You a Theologian?

Some scriptures are so simple that it takes a theologian to make them difficult.

Have you ever forgiven God? If so, it was useless (Romans 8:28).

Never give people a piece of your mind. You may not afford to lose it.

He who calls the shots has to take the shots.

To forgive means to forgive the inexcusable in others as well.

To receive God's forgiveness, we must realize that He knows us better than we do.

Often I am concerned about what I would do in a certain situation, but I know that Jesus said, "My grace is sufficient for thee" (2 Corinthians 12:9).

D. L. Moody was asked if he had the grace to die. Mr. Moody said, "Right now I'm just praying for enough grace to preach three more weeks in Cincinnati." (Same verse in 2 Corinthians 12:9: "My grace is sufficient for thee.")

I HAVE A POSITIVE ATTITUDE. IF I CAN'T KILL OR GET RID OF A FLY, I TAKE SOLACE IN KNOWING THAT IN TWENTY-ONE DAYS OR LESS, IT WILL BE DEAD.

Barney Fife was told that the only thing to fear is fear itself, and he said, "Well, that's what I have—fear itself."

Meet the "Tator" family:

This is Dick Tator: he is the daddy, self-appointed leader of the church, heads all committees, feels very important; he just dictates and never works.

This is Emmy Tator: she is the mother, never has any thoughts of her own, just imitates, always seconds the motion of someone else. She is active in all phases of church work, just imitating.

This is Hezy Tator: he is the oldest son, goes to college. When he is asked to do anything, he just hesitates. He feels he isn't qualified to do any job, always doing something. He just hesitates out of doing anything.

This is Carmen Tator: she is the daughter and sits on the back row at Sunday school, church, and training union. She commentates on everything and everybody.

This is Speck Tator: he is in high school. When asked to take part in programs or at parties, he says no. He will just watch. He never takes part. He just spectates.

This is Grandma Agi Tator: this is the oldest member of the family, grandma Agi Tator. She's been in the church forty years, doesn't believe in any changes at all, is against anything new for the church, believes in doing things the same old way, continually agitates the whole church and keeps things stirred up.

And this is Sweet Tator! This is the ideal member of the church [...] takes part and supports the whole church program, never says no, is generous with time and talents. Never dictates, imitates, hesitates, commentates or agitates the real Christians of our church.

Which Tator are you?

— Sword of the Lord

Now I will glory in the cross

For this I will count the world but loss

There I with Christ was crucified;

His death is mine; with Him I died.

And while I live my song shall be.

No longer I, but Christ in me.

-H. A. Ironside, *Poems and Hymns*, 37

A man came to his preacher and said, "Preacher, I'm in trouble. I'm about to lose my house, my car; they're gonna turn the electricity and gas off; I can't afford food and even more. What shall I do?" The preacher thought a minute and said, "I don't usually recommend this, but my advice is to go home, close your eyes, open your

Bible, and run your finger over the page and stop, and there will be your answer." The next time the preacher saw the man, the man had a Rolex watch, was wearing an Armani suit, had rings on every finger, was driving a new car, and more. Amazed, the preacher asked, "What happened?" and the man said he closed his eyes and ran his finger across the Bible page, and when he stopped and opened his eyes, and there, by his finger, was the answer: "Chapter Thirteen."

The task ahead of us is never as great as the power behind us.

The definition of "failure" is "succeeding at the wrong thing."

Is what I'm living for worth Christ dying for?

Growing up, I had a drug problem. My mama drug me to church every week.

SHARE THE JOY, DOUBLE THE JOY;

SHARE THE PAIN, HALVE THE PAIN (ROMANS 12:15).

When God answers prayer, He pleases us. When we wait, we please Him.

Condemnation pushes us down. Conviction pushes us up.

David went to Goliath "in the name of God." Make sure everything you do can be done in His name.

YOU'RE NOT AT THE MERCY OF THOSE WHO RAISED YOU. YOU HAVE A HEAVENLY FATHER WHO IS ABOVE ALL.

Four preachers were discussing the end times. One said, "I am an amillennialist." The second said, "I am a mid-tribulationist." The third said, "I am a pre-millennialist." The fourth said, "I am a pan-millennialist." The other preachers asked, "What is that?" The fourth preacher replied, "I believe that, somehow, it is all going to pan out."

Did you hear about the man who prayed, "God, give me patience and give it to me now!"

DPP: don't park at the point of your pain.

Reproof: a difficult circumstance that God allows in your life in order to restore fellowship with Him.

People spend about 25 percent more when they have a credit card than when they spend cash: "The borrower is servant to the lender" (Proverbs 22:7).

On investing: the best time to plant an oak tree was twenty years ago. The next best time is today. Note: Jesus spoke on money and possessions more than any other subject.

Did you hear about the two skunks
that went to church?

They had a "pew" all to themselves

Chapter Twenty-Three

Give It to God

Don't be a clod. Start giving to God.

You can't take it with you. You've never seen a hearse pulling a U-Haul.

Sarcasm is anger's ugly cousin.

The angry man opens his mouth and closes his eyes.

Eisegesis: learning line upon line, precept upon precept. Isogesis: taking a line out of context to support your own pet doctrine.

If you're not completely happy, remember that even the creation groans.

"If your lips would keep from slips, five things observe with care: of whom you speak, to whom you speak, and how and when and where."

Nobody's happy all the time—you're not expected to be. But you're to have joy all the time. The Bible says, "Rejoice in the Lord *always*: and again I say, Rejoice" (Philippians 4:4).

HOW CAN WE DEVELOP FAITH?

- BE SATURATED IN THE WORD
- BE SEPARATED FROM SIN
- BE DEDICATED TO THE SON
- BE ACTIVATED BY THE SPIRIT

Never forget the people you pass on the way up; you may meet them again on the way down.

Is God your steering wheel or your spare tire?

An Indian went to a psychiatrist. He said, "Doctor, I keep having these nightmares.

One night, I dream I'm a teepee, and the other night, I dream I'm a wigwam." The doctor replied, "I know your problem; you're too tense" (tents). You got it before the parenthesis, didn't you?

G♥d's plaN f♥R y♥uR lifE was c♥NcEivEd iN l♥vE.

Be careful about blaming hurricanes, massacres, pandemics, etc., on God because both good and bad people die in those events (Proverbs 3:5).

I have two books, ***When Bad Things Happen to Good People*** *and* ***When Good Things Happen to Bad People,*** *and it all boils down to this: we will never know this side of heaven.*

Practice makes perfect.

Mark Twain: "It's not what I don't understand in the Bible that bothers me. It's what I do."

Some are against long hair on men, but they have a long tongue. Some are against short pants, but they have a short temper. "An hypocrite with his mouth destroyeth his neighbour" (Proverbs 11:9).

The power that raised Jesus from the dead is the same power to live every day.

ALL THE WITNESSES WHO SAW THE RESURRECTED JESUS, IF GIVEN SIX MINUTES IN COURT, WOULD TAKE OVER FIFTY HOURS!

We can do nothing to earn it, lose it; all we can do is receive it.

Through the Bible, we have on the earth our origin, our operation, and our outcome.

"Set goals for yourself and desires for others" (Adrian Rogers).

Children brought up in church are rarely brought up in court.

Followers fit in. Leaders stand out.

Old African proverb: to run fast,

run by yourself. To run far, run with others.

They had a fight at the local candy store. Two suckers got licked.

There is no security in heaven. Your security is in Jesus.

Jesus gave Himself for me so He could give Himself to me so He could live Himself through me.

Gambling: one person's profit and pleasure at another's pain and loss.

YOU TEACH PEOPLE MORE BY YOUR ACTIONS THAN BY YOUR WORDS.

You can't serve God unless you serve others.

Chapter Twenty-Four

Arguing?

If people disagree with you, try to find a way to agree with them quickly in order to avoid a back-and-forth argument.

When two people argue over Scripture, both lose, and the devil wins.

We can't ask God:

- for help—if we are not making any effort

- for strength—if we have the strength we are not using

- for guidance—if we are ignoring the guidance we now have

- for faith—when we are afraid to act on what we already know

- for forgiveness—if we continue hating someone

- for mercy—if we intend to commit the same sin again

To do nothing is tiresome because you can't stop to take a rest.

When God says, "Come," He goes out to meet us. When He says, "Go," He goes with us.

I knew a doctor who was married to a dentist. I called them a "pair-o-docs" (paradox).

Wrong is wrong, even if everyone is doing it. Right is right, even if no one is doing it.

I had a college professor who claimed he was always right and never made a mistake, but one day I noticed a bottle of Wite-Out on his desk. He had no answer.

DO YOU KNOW ABOUT LEIGH RICHMOND? HE DROPPED A TRACT ON THE PAVEMENT IN ENGLAND AND PRAYED THAT A SINNER WOULD PICK IT UP.

ONE DID PICK IT UP. HE CARRIED THE TRACT TO RICHMOND IN PRISON AND WAS CONVERTED, AND HE WROTE THE *PILGRIM'S PROGRESS,* WHICH TURNED MILLIONS TO RIGHTEOUSNESS. THE BOOK IS SECOND ONLY TO THE BIBLE IN SALES OVER THE YEARS. THE MAN WAS JOHN BUNYAN.

It was not raining when Noah built the ark.

A miser isn't much fun to live with, but he sure makes a wonderful ancestor.

Be an organ donor. Give your heart to Jesus.

IT IS HARD FOR GRATITUDE AND DISCONTENT TO LIVE IN THE SAME HEART.

A drowning man can't save another drowning man.

Blessed are those who mourn, not those who moan.

You don't come to church to worship; you bring the worship.

We are defined by who we are in Christ, not by our lifestyle.

I stepped into the woods to do some hunting. I saw another hunter. I asked, "Is there much good hunting in these parts?" He said, "Oh yeah, but there's very little finding."

People say, "Get right with Jesus; you may die." I say, "Get right with Jesus: you may live!"

THE BIBLE IS A SUPERNATURAL, SPIRITUAL, SOVEREIGN, SURVIVING, SUSTAINING, SUPERCHARGED BOOK ABOUT MY SAVIOR.

The Holy Spirit never leaves a desiring vessel unfilled or unused.

You can never give kindness too soon because you never know when it is too late.

Always forgive your enemies: it annoys them so much.

FORGIVENESS IS THE SWEETEST REVENGE.

"Miser" and "miserable" come from the same root Greek word *eleeikos*.

Easter: when the sun came up, the Son was up.

Three nails four your sin.

Jesus is alongside you, arm in arm, like a good friend. He's behind you, helping you, ahead of you, showing you the way, below you, carrying your worry, and He is above you, illuminating your path.

The road to hell is paved with good intentions.

When I was a teenager, I had a job, and the boss told me I did the work of three men: Curly, Larry, and Moe.

Have you heard of the law of cancellation? Example: one child says, "Tommy is so stupid," and Billy says, "Yes, but he sure does try hard." One child says, "Jane is so ugly," and Susan says, "Yes, but she wears such nice clothes." One child says, "Ralph is so slow on the football field," but Tommy says, "Yes, but he sure is a good guitar player." The law of cancellation: try it someday.

Pop Quiz 4. Chapters 19-24

Answers at the Bottom

1. Let your smile be:
    a. A window of hope
    b. A display that you are up to something sneaky
    c. A sign that you don't have a clue
    d. A sign that you know something I don't know

2. God wants our money because:
    a. He has been hit hard by inflation
    b. Someone stole His wallet
    c. He knows it wants us
    d. He's heard that the stock market is about to take a downward turn

3. Your prayers to God are answered:
    a. Depending on His mood
    b. Only if you pray on your knees
    c. If you make a deal with Him
    d. "Yes," "no," and "wait"

4. Most people who fly from _____ usually leave a forwarding address.
   a. New Jersey
   b. a single-engine plane
   c. temptation
   d. \Ireland in the winter

5. Why do many people open their mouths?
   a. To espouse gossip
   b. To disrupt the sermon
   c. To exchange feet
   d. All of the above

6. Jesus is the only person ever who could call Himself:
   a. A good magician
   b. One who could get away with a lie
   c. Humble
   d. One who truly embraced all religions

7. According to research, most habits can be broken:
   a. In thirty days
   b. In sixty days
   c. With a big bribe
   d. By doing so much that you get tired of it

8. Everything in your life happens to _____ us to the image of God.
   a. twist
   b. conform
   c. counterfeit
   d. confound

9. Jesus said in 2 Corinthians 12:9,
   a. "If you get in trouble, you're on your own."
   b. "You can listen to Satan when he makes sense."
   c. "My grace is sufficient for thee."
   d. "Troubles happen to destroy our faith."

10. The definition of "_____" is "succeeding at the wrong thing."
    a. failure
    b. success
    c. goofiness
    d. comedy

Answers: 1. a, 2. c, 3. d, 4. c, 5. c, 6. c, 7. a, 8. b, 9. c, 10. a

When I was leaving home, I asked what kind of day he was going to have and he said "ruff"

Chapter Twenty-Five

Who Was Really Ignorant?

It's interesting how ignorant my parents were when I was a teenager, but when I got older, how wise they became!

Fathers: your children's idea of God is influenced by you.

As adopted, we have all the privileges of Christ.

I asked a guy the definition of "apathy," and he said, "Who cares?"

God does not cuss, but He loves people who do.

Be aware that sinners can recognize your religiosity.

A real Christian loves sinners but is wrongfully offended by their presence.

Parable: a story that makes a point to help you remember the point.

A PREACHER HEARD A CHURCH MEMBER SAY THAT HE JUST COULDN'T MEMORIZE SCRIPTURE BUT KNEW ABOUT A THOUSAND JOKES. IF YOU MEMORIZE ONE SCRIPTURE A DAY, DO YOU KNOW HOW MANY YOU WILL KNOW IN A YEAR? I USED THE BACKS OF OLD BUSINESS CARDS TO WRITE ON, OR YOU CAN EASILY CUT 3 × 5 CARDS OUT AND WRITE A SCRIPTURE ON ONE SIDE, THE REFERENCE ON THE OTHER, AND TEST YOURSELF ALL DAY.

When I was leaving home, I asked my dog what kind of day he was going to have, and he said, "Ruff."

Don't just read your Bible; study it.

"A swarm of Flys"

Fly from self and fly from sin.
Fly the world's tumultuous din.
Fly its pleasures, fly its cares,
Fly its friendship, fly its snares.
Fly the sinner's hastening doom.
Fly the scope the wrath to come
Fly to Jesus, He's the road
Fly to Him, alone to God
Fly through mercy's gracious seat,
Fly 'til sorrow's last retreat
Fly to Christ in deepest grief
Fly and you shall find relief.
Fly and let your wings be love
Fly and stretch your flight above:
Fly while life and grace are given.
Fly from hell and fly to heaven.

—Author unknown

Causes of failure:

- I didn't know you were in a hurry for it.

- That's not my department.

- That's not my job.

- I f♡RG♡T.

- I didN'T ThiNk iT was imp♡RTaNT.

- I didN'T GET aR♡UNd T♡ iT.

- I wasN'T hiREd T♡ d♡ ThaT.

- I Th♡UGhT iT was G♡♡d EN♡UGh.

- ThEy will NEVER N♡TiCE iT.

　　　　　　—Sw♡Rd ♡f ThE L♡Rd

"Prayer is a sensible affectionate pouring out of the heart of soul to God through Christ Jesus" (John Bunyan).

Pray as if your life depends on it (your spiritual life does).

Why is prayer often the last resort?

Many people don't know that I was engaged to a girl with a wooden leg, but she broke it off.

Prayers should not be like the oxygen masks in a plane that you only use in case of emergency.

Dusty Bibles lead to dirty lives.

WHATEVER GOD GIVES YOU TO DO IS THE BEST PREPARATION FOR WHAT HE WANTS YOU TO DO NEXT.

Jesus's last act was winning a soul; His last command was to win souls, and His last prayer was for the forgiveness of souls.

The drinking man steps up to the bar, places his glass on the bar, and tells the bartender, "Fill it up." Then he drives to the gas station and tells his friend, "Get out and fill it up." Three days later, the cemetery superintendent tells his workmen, after the casket has been lowered into the grave, "Fill it up."

Twelve things to learn:

1. The value of time

2. The need for perseverance

3. The pleasure of serving

4. The dignity of simplicity

5. The true worth of character

6. The power of kindness

7. The influence of example

8. The obligation of duty

9. The wisdom of economy

10. The virtue of patience

11. The nobility of labor

12. The teachings of Him who said, "Learn of Me."

It's not so much the greatness of our troubles as the littleness of our spirit that makes us complain.

Do you have a personal relationship with Jesus or a corporate (church) relationship with Him?

If God had a wallet, your picture would be in there.

The preacher was preaching on surrender. After the sermon, the preacher issued an invitation to come to the altar. One man brought his watch, laid his watch on it, and said, "I surrender my time to God." One man who had been reckless with his money laid his wallet on the altar and said, "I surrender my finances to the Lord." A lady came and said, "I've been doin' too much gossiping, and I want to lay my tongue on the altar," to which the preacher replied, "Well, the altar is only twelve feet long, but you can lay as much on it as will fit."

Take my advice. When you get saved, even if you go all out, start witnessing, carrying around your Bible, never missing church, be careful (but don't compromise), but be careful not to be "too religious" around your unsaved friends. The next thing you know, you will be able to have them visit the church with you. That is tact.

"If you think Christianity flies in the face of reason, then cover your face"

Chapter Twenty-Six

Deliverance from Storms

God may not deliver you from the storm, but He will go through it with you.

No one will fully understand the Trinity, but many use the illustration of their fathers. My father had three identities, but he was one person. He was my "father," my mother's "husband," and my grandmother's "son." Three identities but one person.

Be not a miracle-monger but a Holy Spirit monger, and He will take care of the miracles.

Just for the fun of it: **Webster's Deluxe Edition Dictionary** *(Nichols Publishing Group, copyright 2001)* *defines a miracle as "a supernatural event or happening regarded as an act of God." Amen!* I believe they got it right.

God is looking for those willing to be willing.

"And the Lord God formed man of the dust of the ground, and breathed into his nostrils *the breath of life*, and man became a living soul" (Genesis 2:7). If you sit in a quiet room all by yourself and listen to yourself breathe, even your breath, as you breathe in and out, utters God's holy name: Y-A-H-W-E-H.

Scientists tell us that if you analyze a shovelful of dirt, you will find out it contains the same seven minerals that are contained in the human body. Truly we were made of the dust of the ground (Genesis 2:7).

There are actually hundreds and even thousands of churches in your town: "For where two or three are gathered together in my name, there am I in the midst of them" (Matthew 18:20). Two Christians together form a church (a fellowship).

TOMORROW: IT IS A PERIOD NOWHERE TO BE FOUND IN ALL THE HOARY REGISTERS OF TIME, UNLESS PERHAPS IN THE FOOL'S CALENDAR.

Make every day your "Son-day," but especially Sunday.

The Scriptures are shallow enough for a babe to come and drink without fear of drowning and deep enough for theologians to swim in without ever reaching the bottom.

It is softer on the waves with Jesus than in the boat without Him.

When trouble comes to you and doesn't lead you to God, you sure have wasted a lot of trouble.

The freedom that Jesus gives is not freedom to do what we want but the freedom to do what we ought.

"Venge" means "to punish." "Revenge" means "to punish back," but that is God's job.

An old country preacher once said, "Don't try to get revenge on others. Let God do it. He can do a better job than you."

Anger is an emotion, not a sin. Example: "Be ye angry and sin not" (Ephesians 4:26), "God is angry with the wicked every day" (Psalm 7:11). This is called righteous indignation.

"Atonement" is the Hebrew word kaphar, which means "to be at one" (at-one-ment) with God. My sins are covered, both what I think and do.

An oldie but goodie: "Take time to smell the roses."

"IT'S A BEAUTIFUL DAY, DON'T LET IT GET AWAY" (U2, "BEAUTIFUL DAY").

The story of Joseph in a nutshell: "from the pit to the palace."

Do you have a filing cabinet in your mind where you store wrongs that you think were done to you, ready to be opened at a moment's notice? Donate it to Goodwill.

When you're angry, pray, even though it's the time when you feel like praying the least.

TV or not TV─that is the question. I try to watch what I call "moral" TV without all the sex and violence, but then there are those commercials. My cable is a service where you can delete the commercials, but if you don't have that, the best solution I can offer is to DVR and fast-forward through the commercials and use a filter to protect your children.

Be extra sure you're right when you go ahead and extra right when you stop.

Forgiveness is not a one-time event. It is continual.

"Temptation is the tempter looking through the keyhole into the room where you are living: sin is your drawing back the bolt and making it possible for him to enter" (J. William Chapman).

God writes with a pen that never blots, speaks with a tongue that never slips, and acts with a hand that never fails.

Our temper is one of the few things that improve the longer we keep it and don't lose it.

Two men were being chased by a big black bear. One of them, panting, said to the other, "I sure hope we can outrun this bear," to which the other replied, "All I'm interested in is outrunning you."

DON'T DESPISE SMALL THINGS: REMEMBER, A LITTLE LANTERN CAN DO WHAT A GREAT SUN CAN NEVER DO: IT CAN SHINE IN THE NIGHT.

"Ere a child has reached to seven, teach him all the way

to heaven. Better still the work will thrive if he learns before he's five" (C. H. Spurgeon).

Men are born with two ears and one tongue that they may hear twice as much as they say.

No sermon is ever quite a success, which leaves men satisfied with themselves.

Wanna prepare for heaven? Praise God. We will constantly be doing that there. He deserves it.

In the Old Testament, your sins were covered. Now they are buried in the depths of the sea.

Give God all you have (and don't have), and He gives you all He's got. What a deal!

If you want to get the new, give up the old. He will exchange beauty for ashes (Isaiah 61:3).

God gave us the ability to laugh. When was the last time you had a good, hearty laugh?

Scientists have found that uncontrolled anger releases a chemical from the heart that restricts the flow of blood, constricting your blood vessels and causing high blood pressure and other health problems.

Emerson said that we all boil, just at different temperatures.

"HE THAT WOULD BE ANGRY AND SIN NOT SHALL BE ANGRY ONLY WITH SIN" (JOHN WESLEY).

Anger is not what you're eating. It's what's eating you.

An observer noticed that he did not hear Amish children yelling out loud at each other on the playground. He asked an older Amish man why, and the man said, "It is because they don't hear their parents yelling at each other."

Chapter Twenty-Seven

Being Right Is Right

Be extra sure you're right when you go ahead and extra right when you stop.

FORGIVENESS IS NOT A ONE-TIME EVENT. IT IS CONTINUAL.

"Temptation is the tempter looking through the keyhole into the room where you are living: sin is your drawing back the bolt and making it possible for him to enter" (J. William Chapman).

Men are born with two ears and one tongue that they may hear twice as much as they say.

In the Old Testament, your sins were covered. Now they are buried in the

depths of the sea.

Give God all you have (and don't have), and He gives you all He's got. What a deal!

If you want to get the new, give up the old. He will exchange beauty for ashes (Isaiah 61:3)

God gave us the ability to laugh. When was the last time you had a good, hearty laugh?

EMERSON SAID THAT WE ALL BOIL, JUST AT DIFFERENT TEMPERATURES.

"He that would be angry and sin not shall be angry only with sin" (John Wesley).

Anger is not what you're eating. It's what's eating you.

It is a mistake to suppose that men succeed through success; they much more often succeed through failures.

N♡ MAN EVER REPENTED ♡N his dEAThbEd ♡f bEING a ChRISTIAN.

Faith is not believing that God *can* but that God *will.*

Courage is what it takes to stand up and speak; it is also what it takes, on occasion, to sit down and listen.

Christ died for sin; the believer dies to sin; the unbeliever dies in sin.

"Long prayers injure prayer meetings. Imagine a man praying for twenty minutes, and then asking God to forgive his shortcomings" (Charles Spurgeon).

"God always gives His best to those who leave the choice to Him" (Jim Elliot).

You cannot repent too soon because you know not how soon it may be too late.

THREE SHORT PRAYERS:

1. "LORD, SAVE ME" (PETER).

2. "LORD, HELP ME" (SYROPHENICIAN WOMAN).

3. "LORD, REMEMBER ME" (DYING THIEF ON THE CROSS).

There are no crown-bearers in heaven that were not cross-bearers here below.

It's not your location or your vocation but your devotion.

Today is a blessing of God. Yesterday was. Tomorrow will be.

Y♡u're always spending time, m♡ney, and energy. Spend right.

If God is your Father, do you have His qualities?

Satan's favorite question: "Hath God said?"

If the truth sets you free, then what does a lie do?

Chapter Twenty-Eight

Our Heavenly Home

To dwell there above, with those who we love—my friend, that will be glory. But to dwell here below with those who we know—well, that's a different story.

Prayer is a serious thing. We may be taken at our words.

The devil is never too busy to rock the cradle of a sleeping saint.

Never be afraid to trust an unknown future to a known God.

When you bury the hatchet, never leave the handle sticking out.

Never put a question mark where God has put a period.

"The cure for crime is not the electric chair, but the high chair" (J. Edgar Hoover).

Men are four:

1. *He who knows and knows he knows. He is wise; follow him.*

2. *He who knows and knows not he knows. He's asleep; wake him.*

3. *He who knows not and knows not he knows not. He's a fool; shun him.*

4. *He who knows not and knows he knows not. He is a child; teach him.*

An oldie but goodie: spare the rod—spoil the child.

NEVER BE MAD AT GOD. HE IS THE ONLY ONE WHO CAN HELP YOU.

There is no one so bad he cannot be saved and no one so good he need not be saved.

The worst form of badness is human goodness when human

goodness becomes a substitute for the new birth.

There are those who can preach the gospel better than I can, but there is no one who can preach a better gospel than I can.

I put my money under my mattress so that I'll have something to fall back on.

To be angry, be angry:

- at the right person

- at the right degree

- at the right time

- at the right purpose

- right way

    — Bartlett, *Familiar Quotations*

Not being angry when you should be is a sin.

I heard a car salesman say, "Don't give too many choices. It confuses the customer, and he won't make a decision."

God gives us two choices: life or death.

It's hard to keep our mouths shut about the good we do.

Do not mistreat people to get things but use things to bring glory to God.

Do not be afraid of getting older. You're just one day closer to heaven.

ANGER CAN BE GOOD. USE IT WISELY.

This is my personal thought, but I have been in the hospital and have been in a lot of pain but didn't die. If I were about to die, I believe God would have taken away the pain in my mind as I got closer to death in my spirit. "O death, where is thy sting? O grave, where is thy victory?" (1 Corinthians 15:55).

A child learning right and wrong is different from those learning that there is evil in this world.

I worked in an office, and the boss asked me if I sent out the circulars. I said, "No, I couldn't find any round envelopes."

You say, "I'm okay under the circumstances." Under the circumstances? What are you doing there?

When you point your finger at others, most of your fingers are pointed back at you.

Difficulties shouldn't defeat us. They should repeal us.

The best evidence for the truth of the Bible is a changed life.

When the Bible speaks, God speaks.

Your children will not go untrained. They will either be trained by you or the world.

Hate the sin but love the sinner.

IF YOU GOT HURT AT WALMART, WOULD YOU NEVER GO BACK? THEN WHY DON'T YOU GO BACK TO CHURCH?

Do you ask others the best thing to do or the right thing to do?

Rejection should be a hurdle and not your grave.

Chapter Twenty-Nine

Where in the World Are You?

We are to be "in the world." Not "of the world."

WE'RE ON THE SS JESUS CHRIST, BUT THE ENEMY WANTS US TO ABANDON SHIP.

If you don't serve God in the valley, you won't serve Him on the mountaintop.

What you believe in times of trouble determines if you will get out.

People may be against us, but nobody is greater than our God.

Have you ever been in turbulence on a jet flight? It was finally over, wasn't it? This, too, shall pass.

Even in the storm, God remembered Noah (Genesis 8:1). He remembers you too.

What is the only state listed in the Bible? The state where I was raised. After forty days and forty nights, Noah looked out of "the *ark and saw*" (Arkansas) land (Genesis 8:13, NIV). That's about as corny as it gets.

FOUR HUNDRED TIMES, WE READ IN SCRIPTURE, "PEACE WITH GOD." IT IS THE TITLE OF BILLY GRAHAM'S MOST FAMOUS BOOK.

If you are not a child of God, you may not be hostile, but He is.

The definition of "anxious" is to be pulled in two directions.

If you're living a life of anxiety, you're not in God's will.

WORK IS THE CHANNEL THROUGH WHICH GOD PROVIDES FOR YOUR NEEDS. IT is He who gives you the power to make wealth (Deuteronomy 8:18).

Look around the world. A nation's prosperity hinges on its spirituality.

We grow when we are kind to those who are unkind to us.

All the good that God has for you when you are saved is like a seed that grows as you water it with the Word.

Patience is how you act while you are waiting on God.

We wait on God with a hopeful expectancy.

When you wait for the things you don't have, think of all the things you waited for when you didn't have them.

GOD'S TIMING IS MUCH BETTER THAN YOURS.

When I worked in construction, the boss asked me why I only carried one board at a

time and the others carried two. I said, "I guess they are too lazy to make two trips."

If it's big enough to worry about, it's big enough to pray about.

If all you talk about is your problems, and if you don't praise Him, you are just rehearsing your problems.

What are you not thinking? (Philippians 4:8)

"You can pick what you ponder" (Max Lucado).

You will never be able to afford to tithe until you tithe.

If Jesus played eighteen holes, the score would be eighteen.

God does not want you to be "independent." He wants you to be dependent on Him.

Nobody can do more to harm me than what I have done to God.

Even if there were no God, what did it cost you? A wonderful marriage, good friends, a sober life, a great family, a good reputation, etc. What would it really cost you to believe in Him? (A meaning to live.)

IF YOUR DNA CODE WERE STRETCHED BACK AND FORTH FROM THE SUN, IT WOULD DO IT 600 MILLION TIMES. SO, THIS JUST EVOLVED, HUH?

The Bible gives no voice for atheism in Scripture. It simply says, "In the beginning, God..." (Genesis 1:1).

If every thought you have thought this last week was flashed across all of our TV sets, would you have to leave town?

God not only gives you life, but He also gives you meaning.

WhEN pEople SEE SomEThiNG REally awESomE, why do ThEy say "My

God" instead of "My Buddha," "My Hare Krishna," "My Muhammad," "My Reverend Moon," etc.? "Thou shalt not take the name of the Lord thy God in vain" (Exodus 20:7). The true and only God.

Writing one scripture helps you memorize it. Try it.

The Christian life is not just difficult. It is impossible apart from the Holy Spirit.

People think that when they're old, all those temptations and thoughts will be gone, but at ninety-four years old, a good Mennonite friend told me, "Brother Ron, Satan never lets up."

If you are right with God, you are right where He wants you to be.

Chapter Thirty

Why Worry?

Our most powerful weapon against worry weighs less than three pounds (our brain).

Know you have a prayer partner (Philippians 4:9). In these days of smartphones, they could be halfway around the world and even speak another language.

Where are you living? In the past, present, or future? (Matthew 6:34)

Teach your children right and wrong, but most importantly, teach them how to hear God.

When I weighed 240 pounds and was a professional wrestler, people used to laugh and point at me at my *expanse*.

The marines are looking for a few good men. God is looking for a lotta good men.

I have been practicing Jesus's policy of "opening not His mouth."

Someone accused me the other day of doing about fifty parts wrong when, in actuality, it was only eight or ten. I didn't say a thing. It didn't matter, someone had told me to do it a different way, and the person he was telling it to didn't matter. It's a hard thing to bite your tongue, but it gets easier as you do it.

ONE WAY TO LEARN NOT TO TREAT PEOPLE IS TO BE MISTREATED YOURSELF.

Easy yes-or-no question. Are you enjoying the abundant life?

Some brag that they could care less what others think of them. An old Amish friend told me that if one or two people say something about you, it's not a big deal, but if a lot of people are

saying the same thing, it's time to do some searching.

On a related note: some people say they don't care if anybody likes them or not. First of all, I think they are lying. Secondly, if nobody liked you, how could you be a witness for Jesus?

I just found out why cannibals don't eat comedians. They taste funny.

"Faith is the substance of things hoped for, the evidence of things not seen" (Hebrews 11:1). If you could see it, it wouldn't be faith.

Self-control sounds like a good phrase, but what about God-control?

Joseph left his coat but kept his character.

The prayer that gets to heaven is the prayer that begins in heaven.

The measure of success is not to look at what you've accomplished but what you've overcome.

Liberalism leads to looseness.

ARE YOU LISTENING? THE NIGHT THE *TITANIC* SANK, ANOTHER SHIP WAS VERY CLOSE, BUT THE WIRELESS OPERATOR HAD GONE TO BED AND DIDN'T HEAR THE DISTRESS CALL. SPIRITUALLY SPEAKING, ARE YOU SAYING, "SPEAK LORD, FOR YOUR SERVANT HEARETH?" OR HAVE YOU *GONE TO BED? (OUR DAILY BREAD,* VOL. 66, DECEMBER 8, 2021).

"Revive" or "vive"? "Wilt thou not revive us again: that thy people may rejoice in thee" (Psalm 85:6). In order to be revived, you first have to be "vived" (made alive through Christ). Have you been "vived"?

To believe in heaven is not to run away from life; it is to run toward it.

We ought to be living as if Jesus died yesterday, rose this morning, and is coming back this afternoon.

When you're saved, God doesn't fix you to where you can't sin anymore but where you can't sin and enjoy it.

Jed Clampett met an oil sheik with 800 wives. When asked what he thought about, he paused a moment and said, "With that many wives, when you get home from work, you ought to be able to find at least one of them in a good mood."

"What seems foolish to many may be faithful to God" (George Washington). For instance: dipping in the Jordan seven times, allowing Jesus to put mud and spit on your eyes, marching around the enemy's camp while singing, whittling down your army from 32,000 to 300 in order to face a larger enemy, going out to fight a nine-foot-tall giant with only a slingshot, etc.

Paul said the first piece of the Christian's armor is not a physical weapon but the truth.

You may be fooled or taken once or maybe twice, but if it continues to happen over and over again, you need to do some soul searching.

When you are not afraid of dying, only then can you live.

Have you heard of the Mason–Dixon line? That is the point at which "youse guise" becomes "y'all."

SATAN IS THE FATHER OF ALL LIES. WHEN YOU LIE, ARE YOU DOING THE WORK OF YOUR FATHER?

If there are "white lies," are there "black truths"?

Do you take your Bible to church? If not, how do you write notes beside scriptures or highlight them when you can only see them on a big screen?

Definition of "spin": to shade the truth to the point that it sounds like the truth but is really a lie.

DEFINITION ♡f 'EG♡TIST': S♡ME♡NE

who is me-deep in conversation.

Many times, when we ask for forgiveness for ourselves or others, even if we don't feel forgiven, we know that God is faithful to forgive us (1 John 1:9). Even if you don't mean it, say it enough, and you will.

"Faith is the substance of things hoped for" (Hebrews 11:1). If you could see it, it wouldn't be faith. It would be proof.

We live by faith, not by sight for proof.

Translations: *exact equivalency* is a word-for-word translation such as the 1611 King James Version or the New King James Version. *Dynamic equivalency* is a paraphrase in some form or another. It translates thoughts instead of words. Whatever is best for you, at least read one.

Whenever Jesus was tempted, He used the phrase "It is written" and the passage (all from Deuteronomy). As New Testament

Christians, our passage to use is one of the first I ever memorized, 1 Corinthians 10:13:

There hath no temptation taken you but such as is common to man: but God is faithful, who will not suffer you to be tempted above that ye are able; but will with the temptation also make a way to escape, that ye may be able to bear it.

AS GUYS, WE CALLED IT "THE GIRLS, THE GOLD, AND THE GLORY."

Is your spiritual life in "park" or "drive"?

I had two girlfriends, Katie and Edith. I couldn't decide which one to marry, so a friend said to me, "Ron, you can't have your Katie and Edith too."

We often surprise ourselves (and others) with what we say, but it is no surprise to God. He knows every word before we speak it (Psalm 139:4).

THE M♥ST H♥PEFUL VERSE IN THE

Bible: "With G♥d, all things are possible" (Mark 10:27).

We tell the truth. Jesus *is* the truth.

I asked a guy, "When rain falls, does it ever get up again?" He replied, "Yes. In dew time."

The word "Bible" (Greek: *biblos*) means "book," but ours also says "holy."

Christians die from malnutrition spiritually if they don't stay in the Word daily.

The Bible gives us Jesus daily (John 6:35), the bread of life.

In John 6:35, He is also called "the bread of heaven."

WHEN WE FISH FOR FISH, WE TAKE THEM OUT OF A BEAUTIFUL LIFE TO DEATH, BUT WHEN WE FISH FOR MEN, WE TAKE THEM OUT OF DEATH TO A BEAUTIFUL LIFE.

The more you like yourself, the

more likable you will be.

Aristotle said, "A friend is a single soul living in two bodies."

If the outlook looks glum, be not dismayed: the *uplook* is very bright.

"Even so, come, Lord Jesus. The grace of our Lord Jesus Christ be with you all. Amen" (Revelation 22:20–21).

Pop Quiz 5.
Chapters 25-30

Answers at the Bottom

1. Does God cuss?

    a. Only when His wife burns the toast

    b. When He hits His thumb with a hammer

    c. No

    d. When it rains on His picnic

2. Parable: a story that makes a _____ to make a point.

    a. lie

    b. joke

    c. soliloquy

    d. point

3. When I was leaving home this morning, I asked my dog what kind of day he was gonna have, and he said, "_____."

    a. Lonely
    b. Active
    c. Lazy
    d. Ruff

4. If God had a _____, your picture would be in there.

    a. garbage can
    b. deep hole
    c. wallet
    d. blazing fire

5. God may not deliver you from the storm, but He will _____.

    a. cross His fingers and wish you luck
    b. throw you a life preserver
    c. call the coast guard
    d. go through it with you

6. The freedom that Jesus gives is not the freedom to do what we want, but the freedom to do as _____ want(s).

    a. I
    b. your spouse
    c. the devil
    d. He

7. What is one of the few things that improve the longer we keep it?

    a. Our car
    b. Our sack lunches
    c. Our temper
    d. Our bodies

8. Spare the rod, _____ the child.

    a. improve
    b. admire
    c. spoil
    d. display

9. You should be enjoying the _____ life.
    a. abundant
    b. bad luck
    c. sickly
    d. convivial

10. Who is an egotist?
    a. Someone who is always concerned with others
    b. Someone you can count on when you're down
    c. Someone who is me-deep in conversation
    d. A good listener

Answers: 1. c, 2. d, 3. d, 4. c, 5. d, 6. d, 7. c, 8. c, 9. a, 10. d

"Surely I come quickly. Amen. Even so, come, Lord Jesus" (Revelation 22:20).

The End

Jesus is the bread of life, so don't be loafing around.

Bibliography

All-American Church Hymnal. Eleventh edition. Nashville, TN: John T. Benson Publishers.

Bartlett, John. *Familiar Quotations*. Boston, MA: Little Brown Publishers, 1980.

Brontë, Charlotte. *Jane Eyre*. Carleton, 1864. Digitized 2007. www.books.google.com/books?id=lSMGAAAAQAAJ.

Brontë, Emily. *Wuthering Heights*. London, UK: Faber & Faber, 2017. www.books.google.com/books?id=svOlDgAAQBAJ.

Elliot, Elisabeth. *A Chance to Die: The Life and Legacy of Amy Carmichael*. Ada, MI: Revell, 2021. www.books.google.com/books?id=Oy8TEAAAQBAJ.

Ironside Henry. *Poems and Hymns*. Solid Christian Books, 2014. www.books.google.com/books?id=cZadCwAAQBAJ.

Philip, Howard. *The Life Story of Henry Clay*

Trumbull, Missionary, Army Chaplain, Editor, and Author. Philadelphia, PA: The Sunday School Times Co., 1905. www.archive.org/details/cu31924050584592.

Phillips, Bob. More Good Clean Jokes. Eugene, OR: Harvest House Publishers.

Rogers, Adrian. *Adrianisms: The Collected Wit and Wisdom of Adrian Rogers*. Collierville, TN: Innovo Publishing, LLC, 2015. www.books.google.com/books?id=Lgg-7jgEACAAJ.

Shakespeare, William. *Henry VI*, part 2. New York City, NY: Simon and Schuster, 2014. www.books.google.com/books?id=W_AF-AwAAQBAJ.

Strong, James. *Strong's Exhaustive Concordance*. Ada, MI: Baker Book House, 1987.

Sword Scrapbook. Compiled by Viola Walden. Murfreesboro, TN: Sword of the Lord Publishers, 1969, 1975, 1980.

Warren, Rick. *The Purpose Driven Life: What on Earth Am I Here For?* Grand Rapids, MI: Zondervan, 2012. www.books.google.com/books?id=m3XJ3x0cFsYC.

Webster's Dictionary and Thesaurus. Asbury, IA: Nichols Publishing Group, 2001.

Weigle, Oscar. *Great Big Joke Book.* New York City, NY: Grosset & Dunlap, 1978. www.books.google.com/books?id=fYvTzgEACAAJ.

Almighty Communications

P.O. Box 1243
Abbeville, SC 29620
FaceBook: Almighty Communications
(864) 548-2116

CPSIA information can be obtained
at www.ICGtesting.com
Printed in the USA
JSHW060059090922
30188JS00002B/2

9 781685 564261